MARRIAGE
A decision for life

"...Therefore a man shall leave his father and mother and be joined to his wife, and the two will not be but one flesh?" 6 So they are no longer two, but one flesh. No man separate what God has joined." (Mt19, 3-6)

"Thus the marriage bond has been established by God himself in such a way that a marriage concluded and consummated between baptized persons can never be dissolved" (CCC#1640)

RICARDO LORA

With due ecclesiastic license:

Nicolás de Jesús Cardenal López Rodríguez

Arzobispo Metropolitano de Santo Domingo
Primado de América

No. 43.071/2012   4 de junio de 2012

Señor
Ricardo Lora
Ciudad

Apreciado Ricardo:

Después de leer su libro *"El matrimonio, una decisión para toda la vida"*, el censor me ha comunicado que no hay nada en él contra la fe y por lo tanto puede exhibir la frase "Con la debida licencia eclesiástica".

Me comenta el censor que: *"No se trata de un libro teórico sobre el matrimonio y la familia sino de un libro testimonial en el que el autor nos presenta lo que ha sido su matrimonio y su familia gracias a su fe firme y sostenida en todo momento... En tiempos de tantos ataques al matrimonio y a la Institución de la familia es reconfortante leer un libro como este de un matrimonio y familia exitosa precisamente por su fidelidad a Dios".*

Le felicito por la decisión y valentía de compartir su experiencia a través de este libro. Quiera Dios que muchos tengan la oportunidad de leerlo y beneficiarse de todo su contenido y de sus oportunos consejos.

Reciba, pues, mi saludo y especial bendición para Ud. y su querida familia,

✝ NICOLAS DE JESUS CARDENAL LOPEZ RODRIGUEZ
Arzobispo Metropolitano de Santo Domingo
Primado de América

NJCLR/ap

DEDICATION

To the Lord for the gift of my wife Elena, my children Manuel, Eileen, Ivette, Angie and my granddaughters Lisette Marie, Amelia Isabel and Mariajosé, who along with Him, have given meaning and beauty to my earthly life.

ACKNOWLEDGMENTS

To God in the Holy Trinity, by His Love, His patience, for His mercy, for His inspiration and His Big Help.

To the Blessed Virgin, my Mother in Heaven, for Her intercession in making this book a reality.

To St. Joseph, patron of the family, for His constant intercession and protection.

To Elena, my dearest wife, who is the human support of our home.

To the friends who read the final draft and gave me a very encouraging response for publication.

To my daughter Eileen, my special thanks for critically reading the initial draft and for her many valuable suggestions. She is the reason that I included the first chapter of the book: You as a human being.

To Larissa, who lovingly performed the layout of the book and helped with the grammar.

To Ester Hernandez who designed the front and back cover of the book.

To Lisette Marie Lora, my first granddaughter, who helped in the design and final presentation of the book for publication.

To my kids and granddaughters, with whom Elena and I formed this home that is the result of each and every one of us.

FOREWORD

"For the tree is known by its fruit."

This is a book for men and women, single and married, Christian and non-Christian, to be read by yourself or with your spouse.

It's a book that not only shows us the experiences and thoughts of one person – because of these exist as many as there are persons in the world- but the Truth of the Gospel of Jesus Christ as living from the vocation of husband, leader, and father from this man of God and the fruits –his family- that produced a life of obedience, and self-sacrifice… "For the tree is known by its fruit." (Mathew 12:33)

It is an honor for me to express the feelings and reactions that this book has awakened in me. Not only for its great content, but also for the great appreciation I have for Don Ricardo and his beautiful family.

A couple of months ago, he asked me to read his draft and this is part of the message I sent to him regarding his request:

"Two days ago I said to you that I will finish reading your draft by the end of the week. I am ashamed to say it, but I had to read it all at once. To read all your experiences and the gift of wisdom that the Lord has given you was inspiring to me.

I believe that the combination that you make with the teachings of the Church, Sacred Scripture, the Theology of the Body, your life, and your well-founded opinions are brilliant.

I think that it is easy to read for any man, woman or couple in any spiritual level that they may be; especially, if they are seeking the right way to live their marriage and family just as the Lord asks from us. It will also be of great motivation for those who are not yet close to the Lord. It is really very extensive. You see, I couldn't stop reading it so I cheated, and I read it all yesterday -by 2:00 PM I was done.

Your faith, mistakes, and successes will be inspiring and will bring anyone that reads it closer to the Kingdom of God, like it did for me.

There is no doubt that the Lord always works for our good. Your book has motivated me to continue in this path. To strive for holiness within my vocation and to take my family in the only Way that takes us to the fullness as persons, matrimonies, and families. It also motivates me to continue fighting for the institution of the family and to help restore this great Gift of the Lord: the Sacrament of Matrimony."

This book shows parents and future parents the importance of a good preparation for marriage starting with a good formation for our children inside our homes, 'The Domestic Church', where they seek in their future spouses the example they have received at home. This way they can find the right person whom the Lord has destined for them from eternity, and not the first person that crosses their sight with whom they share nothing in common.

This book has brought a lot of memories from the time I was courting my wife. It has awakened and motivated in me a great desire of writing letters to her once more, because that was something I used to do often when we were dating. During our marriage, I have done it very rarely.

I'm sure that every single person that reads this book will have similar reactions that will awaken a great desire for a better marriage in all its aspects.

This is a book from a man that went all in - against all odds- for the Truth and is on his way to his reward.

This is a book that dares, in a very singular way, to call our attention to fallow the plan of a living and loving God that only desires what is best for His children, which is opposite to the political correctness, contrary to what the culture tells us: "live together now, get married later"; "whoever has more toys wins"; "enjoy now, pay later"; "children are an obstacle to our careers," "let's not have any," or "let the nanny take care of them," or even worst, "let the TV take care of them," "I'm a good person"; "I'm a very spiritual person"; "if everybody does it. Why shouldn't I?"; "God only wants to oppress and punish us"; "marriage until death do us part is old fashioned, if it doesn't work let's get a divorce."

This book not only teaches us, but also demonstrates to us, with facts, the contrary of these affirmations. It shows us that in following God's plan we can have real freedom and the fullness of His love in our lives, marriages, and families in which we no longer will have a house, but a home and not only any home but the Home of Nazareth.

It is my great desire that one day I can look back and see that I have done my role as leader of my home at least as half as well as Don Ricardo has done it.

I give thanks to the Lord and Our Blessed Mother for your life, for your family, for your marriage, and for sharing with us all such a great gift that the Lord has given you.

I pray for all who read this book –just as I did– you will have a new infusion of the Holy Spirit, that motivated by Him we can become light for the world, spreading the Good News with our example of holiness. Amen!!!

In Jesus, Mary, and Joseph,

Jorge Cebreros
Transformed Marriages

THE SACRAMENT OF MARRIAGE

Since this book is about marriage, then we wish to start with the information about it which is given to us by the Holy Mother Church in the Catechism of the Catholic Church (CCC).

Marriage is one of the seven sacraments of the church, located within those engaged in the service of the community.

Two other sacraments, Holy Orders and Matrimony, are directed towards the salvation of others; if they contribute as well to personal salvation, it is through service to others that they do so. They confer a particular mission in the Church and serve to build up the People of God. (CCC#1534)

Jesus elevated marriage to the dignity of Sacrament:

"The matrimonial covenant, by which a man and a woman establish between themselves a partnership of the whole of life, is by its nature ordered toward the good of the spouses and the procreation and education of offspring; this covenant between baptized persons has been raised by Christ the Lord to the dignity of a sacrament." (CCC #1601)

It is recommended that the marriage be made within the Eucharistic celebration:

"In the Latin Rite, the celebration of marriage between two Catholic faithful normally takes place during Holy Mass, because of the connection of all the sacraments with the Paschal mystery of Christ.[120] In the Eucharist the memorial of the New Covenant is realized, the New Covenant in which Christ has united himself for ever to the Church, his beloved bride for whom he gave himself up.[121] It is therefore fitting that the spouses should seal their consent to give themselves to each other through the offering of their own lives by uniting it to the offering of Christ for his Church made present in the Eucharistic sacrifice, and by receiving the Eucharist so that, communicating in the same Body and the same Blood of Christ, they may form but "one body" in Christ." (CCC # 1621)

The two parties of the marriage covenant must express freely the consent that is received by the priest or deacon who assists at the celebration.

Let's see how this is explained in the catechism:

"The consent by which the spouses mutually give and receive one another is sealed by God himself.[141] From their covenant arises "an institution, confirmed by the divine law, . . . even in the eyes of society."[142] The covenant between the spouses is integrated into God's covenant with man: "Authentic married love is caught up into divine love." (CCC# 1639)

The marriage union is for life. Nothing and nobody can ever dissolve it:

"Thus the marriage bond has been established by God himself in such a way that a marriage concluded and consummated between baptized persons can never be dissolved. This bond, which results from the free human act of the spouses and their consummation of the marriage, is a reality, henceforth irrevocable, and gives rise to a covenant guaranteed by God's fidelity. The Church does not have the power to contravene this disposition of divine wisdom.[144]". (CCC# 1640)

I suggest you read everything that the Church teaches on this Sacrament in the Catechism of the Catholic Church.

Let us thank God, our Heavenly Father, for this Holy Sacrament.

INTRODUCTION

Elena, my wife and I had a courtship relationship for 4 years, and upon concluding this book, we have had 45 years and 6 months of marriage. Moreover, the Lord gave us five children: Manuel, Jennifer, Eileen, Ivette and Angie. So far, we also have three granddaughters: Lisette Marie, Amelia Isabel and Mariajosé.

The Lord permitted us to be with Jennifer for only eight months. She is the first of our family to get to heaven.

I can tell you, we have thoroughly enjoyed the time that God has given us together both in courtship and in marriage.

How many blessings have the Lord our God and the Blessed Virgin Mary our Mother in Heaven bestowed upon us!

Marriage is an enjoyable and rewarding experience when you live it with responsibility, and it is based on faith.

Listen to this, when Elena and I are together, we have always slept in the same bed, and I have never had to sleep by her feet. [1]

(1). Elena and I are Dominicans. In our country there is the expression: "Sleeping by the feet" which means that the couple went to bed angry with each other and therefore, the wife asks the husband to lie in such a way that his head lies alongside her feet, and her feet, alongside his head.

By this, I want to say that we never go to bed being angry; we always resolve any situation before going to bed.

Elena and I come from Catholic households that practice their faith thanks be to God, and we continue in our marriage the practice of our religion to the fullest.

Are we equal? Of course not! We are totally different.

Do we think alike? Of course not! Everyone has their point of view and expresses it fully.

Have we had differences? Of course! But everyone can explain what he or she believes of a specific situation.

Have we been happy and do we still love each other? As you can never imagine!

Our love has been consolidated over time and has grown to fill, fully, our bodies and minds.

How could our marriage not be successful if from the engagement, we decided to build it on Jesus, the strong rock that holds firmly everything built upon Him and His teachings (read Matthew 7, 21-27).

In addition, we have been very aware of the exhortation that Jesus made to us, "be holy as my heavenly Father is holy." (Mt5, 48).

It is true that we fully deal with meeting our personal and family needs without neglecting at all to obtain our ultimate goal: the salvation of our souls.

We must have it quite clear; nothing should interfere with obtaining the crown with which the Lord awaits for us at the end of our earthly life.

In this book, Elena and I want to share our experience together as fiancés and in marriage.

I will try to be as explicit as possible, so that you can pick, and if you want, to apply in your own lives and relationships of courtship and marriage, many of the things we used to achieve the courtship and marriage that we have enjoyed for so many years.

I do not know if they could work for you as they did for us, but I'm sure that they could be helpful when observed and practiced with love and great faith after making the modifications and variations you may consider relevant.

I will present the topics included in this book taking into account this double dimension:

- As if they only depended on our human reality, on our ability, skill, and knowledge.

- As if they only depended on God, His love and mercy for us.

That our reason may help us, and that God may bless and guide us with His Holy Spirit.

Chapter I.
YOU, AS A HUMAN BEING

The human being is the most intelligent of all living creatures.

It is a being endowed with reason that interacts with the surrounding environment.

In order to establish a good relationship with another person, or a particular group: family, school, work, church, in society in general, there must be harmony in our whole person.

We must love ourselves and accept ourselves as we are with our own individuality.

Be secure, satisfied, and happy with us.

When this happens, we will be prepared for our life in relationship with ourselves and with others.

What can help a human being the most to achieve a sound balance of his personality, to have high self-esteem, is to recognize and accept that he is God's beloved son.

Yes, it is a reality for all. It is the source of our greatest dignity as human beings, knowing that we were created in the image and likeness of God both as men and women.

"God created man in his own image, in the image of God he created him, male and female he created them."[218] Man occupies a unique place in creation: (I) he is "in the image of God"; (II) in his own nature he unites the spiritual and material worlds; (III) he is created "male and female"; (IV) God established him in his friendship." (CCC #355)

Furthermore, he was made the owner of all creation (Gen1, 26), received the power to name all the animals (Gen2, 19), and was granted the great privilege of making him the partners in the creation of other human beings.

What a big distinction!

We are like the creator of all things: the creator of the universe and everything in it, but sin.

We are all like him, but distinct from each other.

That's the beauty of creation, we are different from all other humans, and we are unique. Nobody is like you now, neither has been before, nor will be after!

But, yes, we are the image of God!

God loves everyone with all his being. He is Love and can not stop loving you.

"Before I formed you in the womb I knew you." (Jer1, 5)

He knows us because He loved us from all eternity.

When our first parents, Adan and Eve disobeyed God and fell into sin (Gen3, 1-23) they were expelled from the Garden of Eden, the gates of heaven were closed; so, they could not eat from the tree of life and have eternal life. (Gen3, 24)

Then God, the Father, sent His Son, Jesus, that by His sacrifice on the Cross, He would reopen the doors of Heaven, and with His teachings, we might know the path that would lead us to the Father's house.

"I am the bread of life, says Jesus. He who eats this bread will live forever." (Jn6, 48 -58)

Jesus is the Tree of Life for all human beings.

So great is the love that our Father has for us. He sacrificed His only Son, so that through Him, we could have eternal life.

Thank you, Holy Father, thank you very much!

We are also children of the Blessed Virgin Mary, our Heavenly Mother.

She loves and cares for us. She intercedes to Jesus for us in order to give us everything that benefits us, spiritually and materially.

She says, as She told Juan Diego, now a saint, "Why do you worry? Am I not here who am your Mother?"

If we create a clear awareness of this reality, that we are children of God, nothing would worry us and we would live as our Father wishes: happy, grateful, and with the certainty that my Father loves me just as I am, without any conditions.

"In the presence of Jesus, we find our true identity, our security and dignity, because we discover who we are: beloved children of God.

In the Eucharist, Jesus gives you His heart. You are very precious to Him. He loves you dearly. He knows you personally. He says: I call you friends. (Jn15, 15)

Because Christ chooses us as His friends, we are called to greater intimacy with Him.

Prayer makes us his intimate friends. So, put your loving gaze fixed on the Eucharist." Blessed JPII (Pope's message to young people about the Eucharist)

I suggest you go to a chapel where Jesus is exposed in the Blessed Sacrament, kneel before Him, pray with great faith, and say with all your heart: Lord, grant me the grace to know I am a child of God.

Only when we hold our reality, to be unique, unrepeatable, when we accept ourselves as we are, when we are fully convinced of being God's beloved children, will we have a strong self-esteem.

Then, we will be prepared to interact positively with another person.

This relationship will be nice, dignified, respectful, and confident.

In addition, we will be aware that the other person is also unique, unrepeatable, and a daughter (son) of God.

"In creating men 'male and female,' God gives man and woman an equal personal dignity."[118] "Man is a person, man and woman equally so, since both were created in the image and likeness of the personal God." (CCC #2334)

It is important to remember that being a child of God grants me, and other human beings who are also children of God, a dignity that I must always protect.

Each of the two sexes is, with equal dignity though in a different way, an image of the power and tenderness of God. (CCC # 2335)

All humans have an innate vocation to love. (CCC # 2392)

In expressing our love, we can not forget that we are children of God. Therefore, we must do it bearing in mind the virtue of chastity.

"The virtue of chastity comes under the cardinal virtue of temperance, which seeks to permeate the passions and appetites of the senses with reason." (CCC #2341)

"Chastity is a moral virtue. It is also a gift from God, a grace, and a fruit of spiritual effort.[131] The Holy Spirit enables one whom the water of Baptism has regenerated to imitate the purity of Christ." (CIC# 2345)

Every human being is called to live out chastity according to their state of life or vocation to which each is called by God: single, married, priest, religious, or celibate.

When we practice the virtue of chastity, we come to understand and appreciate the love in all its dimensions.

"Only the chaste man and the chaste woman are capable of true love." JPII

St. Paul reminds us of some of the virtues of love:

"4 Love is patient and kind, love does not envy, it does not boast, it is not proud, 5 does not proceed with baseness, seeks not her own interest, is not provoked, does not take into account a wrong suffered, 6 does not rejoice in unrighteousness, but rejoices with the truth.7 Love It always protects, always trusts, always hopes, always perseveres." (1Cor13, 4-7)

Keep these characteristics of true love in mind when we try to express it to another human being.

We must never let ourselves be guided by instincts or impulses of the flesh. "The flesh is weak," says Jesus (Mt26, 41), on the contrary, we should be obedient to the guidance of the Holy Spirit who dwells in us:

"19 Do you not know that your bodies are temples of the Holy Spirit who dwells in you and they have received from God?" (1Cor6, 19)

If our guide is the Holy Spirit, then we could avoid falling into one of the sins against chastity.

"Among the sins gravely contrary to chastity are **masturbation, fornication, pornography, and homosexual practices.***" (CCC #2396)*

Another grave sin, related to married life, is infidelity. This refers particularly to adultery.

"Adultery. This word refers to marital infidelity. When a man and a woman, of whom at least one is married, have sexual relations, although occasionally they commit adultery..."(CCC #2380)

Christ condemns even adulterous desires:

"27 You have heard it said: "Do not commit adultery."28 But I say: He who looks at a woman lustfully has already committed adultery with her in his heart." (Mt5, 27-28)

Other sins to be avoided are:

"Lust is a disordered desire or inordinate enjoyment of sexual pleasure. Sexual pleasure is morally disordered when sought for itself, separate from the purpose of procreation and union."(CCC #2351)

"Rape is the forcible violent sexual intimacy of another person." (CCC #2356)

"Prostitution does injury to the dignity of the person who engages in it, reducing the person to an instrument of sexual pleasure. The one who pays sins gravely against himself: he violates the chastity to which his Baptism pledged him and defiles his body, the temple of the Holy Spirit (cf. *1 Cor* 6, 15-20)." (CCC # 2355)

"Deep within yourself, listen to your conscience which calls you to be pure. A home is not warmed by the fire of pleasure, which burns quickly like a pile of withered grass.

Passing encounters are only a caricature of love; they injure hearts and mock God's plan." JPII

We also, can sin:

With our eyes. Let us not look with lust at other human beings.

Jesus tells us:

"29 If your right eye is for you an occasion of sin, pluck it out and throw it far from thee: it is better to lose one of your members than that your whole body be thrown into hell." (Mt5, 29)

With our mind. Having and entertaining, in our thinking, sinful scenes and situations.

With our mouth. Saying offensive words, judging the behavior of other human beings, murmuring, etc.

With our style of dressing. By wearing clothes that leave much of our body bare, or when used very tight to the body.

"The United States Senate reports of the bitter fruit born of the sexual revolution and the modern sexual education that began in the decades of the sixties: 600% increase in teen pregnancies, 300% increase in youth suicides, 13 and 19 years old, 232% increase in youth homicides and 400,000 abortions a year, committed in babies of young girls, less than 19 years old.

Then there's the frightening increase of divorces, births outside marriage, single parent families, AIDS, venereal diseases and a decrease in birth rate in the United States. According to information from the federal Centers for Disease Registry, 72 percent of seniors students in high school have had premarital sex, that is, committed adultery, and 43 million Americans have incurable sexually transmitted diseases (genital herpes, etc.)". (Results of the Hedonistic Sexual Education and Chastity, Father Paul Marx, founder of VHI, April 8, 2011).

The words, directed by Blessed John Paul II to young people in Lourdes on August 15, 1983, should guide all of us who want to experience love and sexuality, following the guidance of God and our Holy Mother Church.

John Paul II, said, "Those who speak of a spontaneous and easy love deceive you. According to Christ, love is difficult and demanding journey. To be what God wants, requires a patient effort, a struggle against ourselves. We must call it by its name the good and evil. "

To resist the temptation to stay pure, we must strengthen ourselves with: constant prayer (the Holy Rosary can help us a lot), with fasting, and the practice of the sacraments.

Confession and frequent reception of the Holy Eucharist are of particular importance to achieve that purpose.

We must always keep in mind that each human being has his own dignity and deserves all of our respect and recognition.

"To be pure, to remain pure, can only come at a price, the Price of knowing God and loving him enough to do His will.

He will always give us the strength we need to keep purity as something as beautiful for Him." Blessed Mother Teresa.

Coming to the end of this chapter, I wish to recommend that you do the meditations necessary to absorb the beautiful reality that you are a child of God.

This is very important before starting a relationship with another person which could be permanent such as a marriage within the Catholic Church.

Finally, I give you the following suggestions:

a) Read, every day, some passages of the Holy Catholic Bible.

b) Familiarize yourself, in general, with the contents of the Catechism of the Catholic Church (CCC).

c) When you're reading this book of Marriage, read also, the # s from 355 to 421 in the CCC.

d) In addition, read about the seven Sacraments of the Church.

e) Visit the Lord in the Blessed Sacrament - go to meet with the Eucharistic Jesus.

May the Lord Jesus, the Holy Spirit, and the Blessed Virgin Mary, help you find your true self: The son of God!

Blessings in your life and a lot of happiness!

Chapter II.
PREPARING FOR MARRIAGE

The most important decisions for us in this world are those that commit us for a lifetime.

The options to give my life to God as a religious, or as a Catholic priest, are lifelong decisions.

Similarly, marriage by the Catholic Church is a decision for life. "Until death do us part" is the commitment of the bride and groom on their wedding day declared before the priest or the deacon, who presides over the ceremony representing the church.

When you think something is for life, you must think carefully and deeply before making a decision that has that implication: forever, till death do us part.

During our existence in this world, each of us makes many decisions, some of which are quite important:

What career do I want to study?

Where do I want to live, in what country? What sport I would like to play as a profession? Etc.

Let's take the case of the professional area in which I want to work.

Let's say, just to exemplify, if I choose to prepare myself for Systems and Computer Engineering.

To achieve this goal, I have to spend 12 years to graduate from high school, then 5 years for the Bachelor of Engineering, 2 years for a Masters in Engineering and 3 additional years for a Ph.D in Engineering.

We're talking about 22 years to have an adequate preparation in the chosen area.

In other areas, it could be more or less time, but let's continue with the chosen career as an example.

Why prepare so well?

To make a lot of money could be the answer, and why would we want a lot of money? To have a good car, good house, to travel wherever we want, etc.

These could be many of the reasons we have to prepare for so long for any given profession.

If we continue asking the why's we do all these sacrifices, and spend so much time getting a good profession, then surely we would conclude that the last reason would be for us to be well prepared to have a home, that is, to have our own family.

If you feel a strong desire to serve God through the priesthood or religious life, then these too are lifelong decisions.

For ease of explanation I will, in what follows, confine myself to the case of persons wishing to marry.

However, I will take for comparison people who choose a sport as a profession.

My attention is greatly drawn to the case of athletes participating in the Olympics.

These athletes spend four years preparing daily for such an important event: very strict regimen of diet, and daily practices of their chosen sport.

They inhibit themselves from many other activities that, while being healthy, could adversely affect their performance in the Olympic competitions.

Sometimes, I think of an athlete like a professional racer whose specialty is the 100 Meter race.

This person spends 4 years of hard and constant preparation to participate in a competition that only lasts about 10 seconds each time, and who could also be disqualified after the first attempt.

I present this extreme situation to emphasize that if the devotion of so much time for something that can last so little is important, how much more then should we spend to prepare for an event that lasts forever: MARRIAGE.

I come from a family of 15 people: my father, my mother, and 13 children - Yes, 13 kids-, but now such families are an endangered specimen.

Economically speaking, my family was very poor and we had many limitations of all kinds.

My father was a master builder (of houses).

In the Dominican Republic, where my wife and I come from, there was that title: Master builder.

A Master builder received the blueprints for a house from an architect and an engineer and was able to build a house or a building.

But there was no continuous work in the construction area, and sometimes for weeks, or even months, there was no income for the family.

Imagine the situation that occurred where there were 15 people who had to eat, be clothed, etc., and no income at all.

On the other hand, and to complicate matters further, my father had children outside of the marriage.

My mother told us that his mother took my father, whom I do not want to accuse or excuse, at 3 years of age to construction sites in order to help in some way and thus be able to get him something to eat.

Meaning that my father only knew that work environment. But in that environment, it was normal for a man to have more than one woman.

That was part of being "macho," an expression that means: to be a real man.

I want to clarify that I'm talking about the Dominican Republic, a Caribbean island, during the years of 1915 to 1964. The latter year, my father died.

Despite that fact, my father taught us how important it was to be honest and responsible.

My mother was a caring person and very religious.

That is, on the one hand, my father with a job that did not guarantee a constant supply of resources for our family's needs and his infidelity to the marriage, and on the other hand, the humanity and piety of my mother.

This marked my life forever.

I relate this preamble of my family because the environment in which I grew up totally affected my life and led me to adopt a resolution when I was about 18 years old that still remains in full force:

"I will do everything possible so that the family that I form will never lack the resources they require to meet our material needs.

My spouse and I, with the children that the Lord will grant us, will practice our Catholic faith as my mother taught us.

In addition, I will be faithful to my wife all my life because I do not want us to live a situation in my home, such as the one my brothers, mother, and I had to live in my mother's house."

Up to now, after more than 45 years of marriage, everything has been fulfilled as I desired it thanks to the invaluable cooperation of my wife and the very generous HELP of our Heavenly Father and the Blessed Virgin Mary, without whose blessings our efforts would have been unsuccessful.

The first thing Elena and I always do before making a decision of any kind is to present it in prayer to the Lord Jesus and the Blessed Virgin.

We are confident that they will guide us in the best course of action for each case. That is our faith.

Chapter IIa.
PREPARATION FOR PRODUCTIVE LIFE

In marriage, we will have to provide financial resources to help fill the needs that arise in it.

In my case, my first thought was to become a professional. I decided in high school, when I was in 12th grade, that I would study Civil Engineering to build houses, as did my dad, but with the title of Engineer.

But in 1960, in the Dominican Republic, there was only one university in the city of Santo Domingo, The State University.

I decided then to join the armed forces to become a pilot, and then obtain permission to study Civil Engineering at the State University, as did one of my older brothers to get the title of economist.

I entered, therefore, into the Military Academy.

After 2 years at that academy, I learned that a private university had been created in Santiago: Universidad Católica Madre y Maestra, UCMM.

I then gave up my military career and moved to Santiago for the purpose of studying at that university.

The UCMM was a private university, and therefore, one had to pay.

In the State University studies were free.

That reality, having to pay for college, was new to me and for all Dominicans.

The economic situation of my family was such that any amount that we had to pay was too much for my dad and me.

But our God is always attentive to the needs of his children.

My mother never stopped praying for me to achieve my goal of study. I also asked the same thing of my God.

The Lord, who always hears the prayer from the heart, acted as follows:

A high school teacher got sick and they called me to teach Algebra.

I had studied in that school and graduated from there with good academic qualifications.

The teacher who became ill knew me and recommended me to the school principal in order to replace her.

So it happened-- I taught for three months.

Bermudez, a liquor firm from Santiago, Dominican Republic, gave 8 scholarships to study at the UCMM.

The scholarships would be awarded to the 8 students that got the highest scores in some tests that would be applied to 32 students selected by the school administration.

Since I had helped the school, replacing the ill teacher, the school principal gave me the opportunity to compete in the challenge to get one of the 8 scholarships.

Meaning that I would be one of the 32 students who would take the exam.

I took it and got a scholarship, so I could realize the dream of studying to obtain a professional degree.

Not as Civil Engineer, as was my desire, but as Business Administrator.

In those years, 1963-1970, the University did not have the engineering careers. In addition, the scholarships were only for Business Administration.

Look, dear readers, how the Lord our God acts when we do our part (I prepared very well in high school), the Lord does his own, if we deliver our projects to Him and place our trust in Him.

I want to tell you of God's intervention in another important moment in my life.

When I had the opportunity to study in the UCMM for the scholarship, I gave myself over fully to study. So, I was getting excellent grades.

I started studying in 1963.

In my second year, the year of 1964, something tragic happened in my house which would affect my family and my studies: my father died.

What a difficult situation!

In addition to the sadness of losing my father, I realized I could not continue in college. I would have to work to help support my home.

I was 4th in order of age, but the 3 older brothers had married and their income was barely enough for the families that they had formed.

We were still 10 siblings along with my mother in her house and with zero income.

In this situation, I spoke with the director of my career. I communicated to him the decision to leave the University in order to work and make some income for my household.

Mr. Manuel Jose Cabral, my director, asked me not to make any decision and to wait for a few days because he wanted to explore some alternatives.

On the third day, Mr. Cabral called me and reported the following: "I spoke with "Poppy" (as they called Mr. J. Armando Bermudez, president of the company which had granted the 8 scholarships to which I referred earlier), and he said that he would give you the equivalent of 2 or 3 scholarships to help support your home and; so, you do not have to drop out."

I had done my part, getting good grades, and my God did His. Glory to God!

So, I completed my first college degree.

To shorten this part of my professional training, I can only say that for my qualifications, I was selected by the University to do a specialization in the United States of America.

The UCMM opened in 1962 and the first class graduated in June 1967.I was part of this first class.

Initially, all the teachers were foreigners. There were some Dominican professionals who collaborated in the teaching of the new University.

That was not the situation that the founders of the university had planned.

So, they created a program to train college professors with the help of international agencies.

I was selected into that program.

I signed a contract with the UCMM to study in the United States and return as a teacher and or administrator of the university.

One of the conditions of the signed contract stipulated that I should work at the UCMM for a time equal to, or greater, than the time employed in obtaining the specialty to which I was sent.

In addition, I got a financial loan from the University that would be passed on to my mother's home on a monthly basis to help while I was out. This was done.

I spent 3 years in the U.S. where I did studies for a Masters and Doctorate degree in Business Administration.

I returned to the Dominican Republic in 1970 and joined the UCMM as professor and director of the School of Business Administration.

My God and I had achieved that goal, Blessed be God!

Chapter IIb.
SEARCH FOR THE SPOUSE,
CONTINUATION OF THE PREPARATION

As I prepared professionally, almost simultaneously, I was making inquiries to find the person who would be my companion for life.

In prayer, I asked my Lord Jesus and the Blessed Virgin to put in my path the person they had chosen for me.

I said to myself that in this, I cannot be wrong because in this area, the decision is forever. Marriage is for life.

Also, what will happen in marriage is so important that you cannot commit an error. So, you must prepare for it with great care.

I must be careful in choosing a career, employment, workplace, and everything associated with the source of income for my future family and me.

These, however, may change over time due to market conditions and the economy in general.

In my case, these varied during my working life: I worked in 3 different places.

In the case of the election of a boyfriend or girlfriend, we must be extremely careful; since, we are talking about finding the person you will share every day, every night, and every year, "until death do us part".

Moreover, this will be the person with whom we will procreate the children that the Lord wants to give us, the person who will help me create the ideal optimal environment in the home that will be formed and where we'll raise our children.

I cannot find adequate words to express the importance I give to this search of that partner for life. What I can say is that after marriage, it is no longer possible to go back - I can no longer change my spouse!

It's not like a job or a profession where I can choose a different one depending on the conditions that arise.

In marriage, the choice of my partner is for life!

So, I reiterate the importance of taking the time to make such inquiries as are necessary, to gather all the information needed and to pray with great devotion and great faith so that our God and the Blessed Virgin put the best possible partner in our path.

You must know that man and woman are physically, anatomically, biologically, physiologically, and emotionally different, among other things; that the family, social, and cultural environment affect the personality, character, behavior, and reaction of each person.

Therefore, we must become familiar with- as much as we can- those factors that will affect our lives as partners.

I did my best to know each and every one of these aspects with the sources that were available at that time in the beginning of the 60's.

I learned that Elena, then, had done something similar.

The first thing that usually attracts our attention to another person is perceived through the senses: physical appearance, voice, gestures, actions, and so on.

We must remember here that this person is a child of God and therefore, we must treat him (her) with the dignity this condition confers to him (her).

One of the measures we must take is to surround and make friends with people who have similar values as ours: moral, family, religious, etc.

"He who has found a friend has found a treasure." (Ecclesiasticus 6, 14)

Of all the persons of the opposite sex with whom you relate, we should try to develop a friendly relationship with the one you prefer in order to know him (her) better.

So that we could know: what attracts him (her), what he (she) enjoys, how he (she) spends his (her) time, who are his (her) friends, etc.

If we like what we have found, we go deeper: Where was he (she) born, who is his (her) family, religion, and so on.

If, on the contrary, what we discover does not encourage us to move forward, then it's best to stop there.

By this I mean, not to reach a dating relationship with someone with whom I already know that I would not like to share my life.

This should be the attitude of a serious and honest search with yourself and the related person.

In the case of Elena and me, I had the pleasure of meeting her maternal grandmother and grandfather. They were neighbors of my family. Elena's uncle was my friend.

My mom and Elena's grandmother, Mrs. Emelinda, were very close. Both were practicing Catholics, and with an incredible goodness and kindness.

How was I to think that a granddaughter of Mrs. Emelinda, Elena, would later be my dear wife?

I was about 8 or 9 years old at that time. This means that Elena would have been 2 or 3 years of age at the most.

How the Lord works! Some 12 or 13 years later, I would see Elena for the first time.

My family, and that of Elena's, had moved to different locations in the city.

I had not heard from Elena's grandmother and Elena's uncle anymore. They had disappeared from my life.

But my God put Elena in my way. There she was, at a corner of the neighborhood where they lived wearing a khaki colored school uniform. What a beautiful vision!

She was with her back towards me. Her golden hair hung down to her waist. I was entranced, admiring her beautiful figure.

When she turned towards me- Oh my God, what a beauty! I felt a feeling, until this moment, unknown to me, of tenderness and protection. Yes, I wished to care for and protect that person - a person who I did not know. I had never seen her before.

That meeting took place a few meters from the house where my best friend lived. So, I went to his home and asked his wife whom that person was.

Elena was still standing in the same place. It seemed that she was waiting for someone. My friend's wife told me that her name was Elena and that she was the sister of a friend, her hairdresser named Gladys.

From that day on, I began to visit my friends more often, hoping to meet Elena.

A few days later, we met at my friend's house. We were introduced, and I shook her hand for the first time.

When I met Elena, I lived in Santo Domingo, because I still was at the Military Academy, as I explained before.

At that time, the beginning of the 60's, we had no phones in our homes, neither at my friends', Elena's family, nor in my house.

There was no cell-phone or computer.

Our only form of communication when we were apart was by mail. But, that was difficult too because at the Military Academy we were very restricted.

So, I did everything possible to have a few days off and when I could get them, I immediately went to Santiago. I looked for my friends and asked them to invite Gladys and Elena to go to a movie or spend a few social moments together.

The social and cultural custom, in those years, was that a young woman had to be accompanied with someone older than she if she wanted to share time with a boy.

That is, Elena and I never went out alone.

Despite these limitations, we got to know each other quite well.

Therefore, I had two main reasons for leaving the Military Academy: the opening of the first private university in the Dominican Republic, the UCMM of Santiago, and the desire to continue knowing more Elena.

Elena's family was like mine: practicing Catholics.

Elena, who was about 15 years old when I started to befriend her, possessed maturity far beyond her age, and also had great moral values.

She had great respect for her parents; she treated all people with great courtesy; especially, those who were elders.

I realized that Elena lived her Catholic faith fully, practicing the sacraments. She was also involved in the ministries of her parish.

She, for example, was part of a Catholic group called *The Legion of Mary*. Elena was the youngest of the group.

The Legion of Mary, among other things, took care to detect families whose children were not baptized, who had not made their first communion, or those whose parents were not married by the Church.

They would also visit the sick and seek out a priest for confession and give them Holy Communion when it was necessary for the patient.

When the Legion of Mary found one of those situations, they sought a way to correct them; whatever were their realities.

I realized that I must deepen my knowledge of Elena because the thought that I could see her greatly pleased me; especially, after a few weeks apart, for I was still living in Santo Domingo.

In this way, I could learn the things she liked to do, which ones did not appeal to her, what she liked to eat, if she had a friend, and so on.

Elena had one friend, a girl like her, who lived next door to her house and she conversed with her on some occasions.

Elena's main friend was her older sister Gladys. She went everywhere with her.

Elena has two younger sisters and one older brother.

Gladys worked at a beauty salon and was much in demand by customers at this and other salons.

Elena helped her on some occasions.

If we like much of what we have learned from the person with whom we are relating, then we could continue deepening the knowledge of that person. Therefore, we should try to start a courtship.

Chapter III.
COURTSHIP, CONTINUATION OF THE PREPARATION

Your choice of your partner for life is and must be of the utmost importance to you.

It should be a search of the mind and of the heart. But be careful; do not guide yourself only by appearances.

At this time, the biblical passage in which the Lord instructed Samuel to anoint a person as king of Israel comes to mind.

"The prophet Samuel was impressed with the first son of Jesse. He was going to anoint him as king and the Lord said: "Do not judge from his appearance... Not as man sees does God see, because man sees the appearance but the LORD looks into the heart." (1 Samuel 16,1; 6-7sg.)

We must not be guided only by appearances. The decision is so important that we should dig deeper in all aspects of our partner.

Also, we should accompany this process with constant prayer.

Remember: It is a decision for life.

After around a year of friendship with Elena, and after we both realized that we felt good with each other, we decided to start a courtship.

Yes, Elena accepted my request to be my girlfriend.

When Elena told me yes, that she accepted to be my girlfriend, I felt so happy that I wanted to shout it to the whole world.

The person who had occupied my mind and heart almost entirely for a year had decided to be my girlfriend. What a feeling of joy! How much happiness embraced my heart!

This occurred on December 19, 1962, at around 6.30pm.

How could I forget, Elena had decided that I too was necessary for her!

Blessed be God and the Blessed Mother!

It had started the stage to know each other so much, that we could say that this was the person with whom we wanted to share the rest of our earthly lives.

Elena, like me, had the purpose of dating very clear: to verify, without doubt, that was the person that the Lord had reserved for me and with whom I wanted to join in marriage for life.

You should also end this relationship if, after starting this phase, you find elements that make you think that this is not the person with whom you would share your whole life.

This is best for both, rather than prolonging a decision of ending an engagement because you do not want to cause suffering to the other.

In the past, for example, I thought it was very hard for a couple to decide to end an engagement after 3 years of having initiated it.

Now, I think it is much better and more honest for the two to do this rather than to continue to the final stage of marriage with a person with whom I do not like to be together forever.

On the other hand, if during the time of courtship - for me not less than one year - I realize that this is the person with whom I want to spend the rest of my life; then, we should enter the stage of knowing each other, as much as we can, in all facets of life, except in the sexual aspect which is reserved only for the stage of marriage.

At this stage, we must try to know in depth: our tastes, what we like or dislike, things that annoy me, or may disturb me about the other, and so on.

This is an important stage and should be lived to the fullest with integrity and responsibility.

By this I mean that the couple must appear before the other, just as they are. Do not hide behind words, gestures, actions, etc. that are not sincere and that distort the true self of that person.

No, it is necessary to show each just as he/she is.

Both should discuss at length all facets of marriage until each one understands what the other likes, or hopes to accomplish at home: what you'd like, or you think of the children, how you would like to educate them, and so on.

Our courtship lasted four years.

I want to clarify from the beginning that during this time we did everything possible to know each other as we were, without deception, without pretense, acting in all situations with the greatest sincerity and naturalness. Telling each other what we liked and what we disliked from the other.

We lived the four years of dating in total chastity.

Elena had it very clear that she would give up her body to her husband only after marriage and that she would only marry in a wedding held inside the Roman Catholic and Apostolic Church.

That was defined from the start.

Therefore, to protect ourselves we avoided lengthy expressions of affection.

Today, many young people wear, during their courtship, a ring on their finger as a promise of chastity between them. They even pray together and choose a day in the week to visit The Eucharistic Jesus in the Tabernacle.

We must not forget that in any condition and stage of our lives, we are assailed by Satan to fall into sin.

We are weak; so, we must strengthen ourselves with prayer, fasting, and the sacramental life; especially, the Sacrament of Penance and the Eucharist.

Sex is a gift from God, but it must be done with love and be open to life. Therefore, it must be reserved for the state of marriage.

The church says:

"Those who are engaged to marry are called to live chastity in continence. They should see in this time of testing a discovery of mutual respect, an apprenticeship in fidelity, and the hope of receiving one another from God. They should reserve for marriage the expressions of affection that belong to married love. They will help each other grow in chastity" (CCC #2350)

This behavior was easy for us for 2 reasons:

a) Elena was a practicing Catholic and I was too.

b) Our families, and in almost all of society at that time, it was customary for the woman to arrive at marriage as a virgin.

This, however, was not required of the man.

But this last part was an erroneous teaching.

The truth is, and we must teach our children, that both men and women must guard their virginity until the time of marriage.

During courtship, we talked about: how many children we would like to have, how to bring them up, the atmosphere we would create at home, the way to dialogue among all, and so on.

We spent a long time thinking and searching on the ideal atmosphere we should create at home in order to achieve the integral development of the children that the Lord gave us.

We were able to get enough information despite the enormous limitations of that time: no libraries, no internet, no computer, etc., only an old house called Lovers of Light that was filled with history books and books about Trujillo the dictator.

When I entered the University, the search for information was a little easier because they created a library, which initially had mainly books for each of the existing programs.

After some time, we had a more or less clear idea of what we could do to create the appropriate environment that would facilitate the welfare and development of children and each of us in our family.

One aspect to which we devoted much time and thought was the role of each one of us in marriage.

We agreed that Elena would stay at home with the children that the Lord gave us.

In our youth in the Dominican Republic during the middle of the 60's, it was customary that only one of the spouses work.

The woman was devoted mainly to the domestic duties at home.

That facilitated the decision Elena and I took.

I can tell you:

-The effort of Elena and me to know each other to the point that we could decide for sure what was best for each one of us;

-The important aid of our God and the Blessed Virgin Mary obtained through constant prayer;

-The delivery of our relationship and our future to the full will of God;

All this gave the desired result for Elena and me:

On December 17, 1966, we joined our lives in holy matrimony.

Praise be to God!   Blessed be our Mother in Heaven!

Let us recall what John Paul II said:

"Chastity is a difficult, long term matter. One must wait patiently for it to bear fruit, for the happiness of loving kindness, which it must bring. But at the same time, chastity is the sure way to happiness."

Chapter IV.
THE MARRIAGE, A DECISION FOR LIFE

Our wedding was celebrated in the Church of Nuestra Señora de La Altagracia in Santiago, Dominican Republic.

The celebration took place within the Holy Mass. Elena and I gave each other the Sacrament of Matrimony by expressing our consent before the priest attending the ceremony who received it and gave us the blessing on behalf of the Church.

Also, we received the Holy Eucharist, making us this way, one body with Christ. (See CCC # s 1621, 1623 and 1630)

Marriage is a union for life.

God established this condition as we read in the Holy Scriptures:

"3 The Pharisees came to him and to test him, they said, "Is it lawful for a man to divorce his wife for any reason? '. 4 He answered, "Have not you read that the Creator from the beginning made them male and female; 5 and said: "...Therefore a man shall leave his father and mother and be joined to his wife, and the two will not be but one flesh"? 6 So they are no longer two but one flesh. No man separate what God has joined." (Mt.19, 3-6)

Our Holy Mother the Catholic Church reaffirms this condition, and in her Catechism (CCC), it says:

"Thus the *marriage bond* is established by God himself, so that a marriage concluded and consummated between baptized persons can never be dissolved. This link is the free human act of the spouses and their consummation of marriage is a reality, henceforth irrevocable, and gives rise to a covenant guaranteed by God's faithfulness. The Church has no power to contravene this disposition of divine wisdom (cf. CIC can. 1141)."(CCC # 1640)

To avoid confusion, when we read that the Church cannot dissolve the marriage, it's good to see why this is said.

I think the best thing to do for the great importance of this issue is to quote the Catechism (CCC) exactly:

"The protagonists of the marriage covenant are a baptized man and woman, free to contract marriage, who freely express their consent. "To be free," means: - Not being under constraint; - not be impeded by a natural or ecclesiastical law" (CCC # 1625)

"The Church holds the exchange of consent between the spouses as the indispensable element that "makes the marriage" (CIC can.

64

1057 § 1). If consent is lacking there is no marriage" (CCC # 1626)

The consent consists in a "human act by which the spouses give themselves to each other" (GS 48.1 cf CIC can. 1057 § 2): "I take you to be my wife" - "I receive you as husband "(*Ritual of the Celebration of Marriage*, 62). This consent that binds the spouses to each other finds its fulfillment in the two "becoming one flesh" (cf. *Gen* 2:24; *Mk*10.8, *Eph* 5.31). (CCC # 1627)

"The consent must be an act of the will of each of the parties, free of coercion or grave external fear (cf. CIC can. 1103). No human power can substitute for this consent (CICcan. 1057 § 1). **If this freedom is lacking the marriage is invalid.**" (CCC # 1628)

"For this reason (or for other reasons that render the marriage null and void [cf. CICcan. 1095-1107]), the Church, after examining the situation by the competent ecclesiastical tribunal, can declare "marriage annulment" namely, that the marriage never existed. In this case, the parties are free to marry, but must meet the natural obligations of a previous union (cf. CIC, can. 1071 § 1, 3).)" (CCC # 1629)

I recommend you read in the CCC, everything about this important Sacrament, so you can create a clear conscience about it.

Marriage is located in Chapter Three: The Sacraments at the Service of the Community, Article 7 The Sacrament of Marriage. (# s1601-1666)

To marry is a decision we should take with all conscience.

But I can say without any doubt in my heart that marriage is the most enjoyable experience; rewarding, interesting, complete, and the most important decision that a person who has this vocation can take.

It is also the most challenging, which we must face.

So, we must go to Marriage equipped with all the "tools". That is, we come to marriage with the knowledge of all important aspects that will influence the family we will form. Thus, we can use them well when the situation arises.

It is of great interest that we always have present that the "best use" we do of each one of the tools will be measured by the degree of satisfaction that we produce in our spouse and to all other components of our family.

There are no words that allow me to emphasize to the degree I want of how essential it is to always have in mind that family is the most important. More important than success, than money, than fame, etc.

So, whatever we do, we must have, as the ultimate earthly goal, the well-being of our family.

Now, we will present the most important skills (tools) to take into account to make possible a pleasant and successful coexistence for all household members.

These tools will be dealt with in chapters IVa to IVi.

Chapter IVa.
COMMUNICATION BETWEEN THE COUPLE AND AT HOME

Communication is the first and the most important tool for Marriage because it will be used and needed with all of the others.

Communication can be verbal and/or written. We will begin with verbal communication.

I must emphasize from the outset that verbal communication is done with our mouth, but that simultaneously involved and sometimes the most influential are the movements we make with our body: hands, facial expressions, like smiles, etc.

The tone of our voice may completely change what our words mean.

Therefore, we must familiarize ourselves fully with all of these elements so that communication can be a helpful tool for the family.

Sometimes we do or say something under the premise that we know what our partner thinks and wants in relation to what we say or do.

Usually, this is not true, much less in the first years of marriage.

It is a wise rule, and I recommend it: Do not assume that we know what our partner wishes, wants, or would do, in any given situation.

As partners for life, you must agree to show yourself as you really are. Never acting or pretending to feign, or submitting a different image other than your own.

They must say frankly: what they like, what they do not like, what they definitely reject, what they think or feel in each of the actions and / or decisions which will be taken during their life together.

We should neither assume that our partner knows what we think, want, or desire in an action or situation. It is better, healthier, and safer to tell him (her) verbally or in writing.

This is necessary for harmony in the home, and it can only be achieved through effective communication.

Remember, the relationship with the other is determined by how you feel about yourself; therefore, your reaction to what the other says or does is largely dependent on your self-esteem.

Love yourself; accept yourself. Be filled with love because nobody can give what he does not have. Then, give it to others.

You and your partner are the image of God, but distinct from each other.

We are all unique. Therefore, accept the other as he (she) is with much love. Do not desire them to be like you; on the contrary, enjoy the differences.

Surely that pleases you that others accept you as you are. Do the same and you will see how pleasant the relationship is with the other person!

Remember what Jesus tells us:

"12 All who want others to do for you, do it for them." (Mt7,12)

For communication or dialogue to be effective, it requires that participants be clear with what everyone wants.

In addition, each of you must seek the welfare of others and other family members in everything you do and / or say, at home or outside it.

You should also observe this rule: When one talks the other listens with attention to what the first one is trying to say.

It is important to try to understand what the speaker wants to say. Just listen, do not try to interpret what you are being told and much less, do not try to guess what the other wants to tell you, never!

The essential thing is to capture what you are being told. If we are not sure, then we should try to clarify it. In this case, we say what we understood and let the speaker confirm or correct it.

Thus, alternating between talking and listening, you will know each other little by little until you reach a point where the dialogue will flow easily between the two.

However deep the knowledge the one of the other may be, never make an important decision that affects the family and / or spouse assuming you already know your partner fully.

Dialogue, of course, takes place in stages prior to marriage: in the process of knowing each other and during courtship.

The same elements must be present in these two stages as well.

Despite our 45 years of marriage, Elena and I, when making a decision, do not assume what the other wants, wishes, or would do, but each one expresses it verbally.

Remember that each person, because of the qualities of being unique and unrepeatable, reacts differently to the same situation or stimulus.

Therefore, it is best to allow each one to express their point of view in any situation in which a family decision will be taken.

It is possible, however, that despite taking into account all the factors involved in dialogue that communication may not flow properly.

For example, one spouse can be very emotionally tied to a particular topic and find it hard to stay calm and able to express a point of view with evenness of temper or serenity.

In such a case, it is best to write what you think regarding the subject matter.

Other situations will arise in which a family member deems it necessary to communicate, in writing, a position with respect to a matter of the home.

In short, the important idea in communication is that no member of the family is deprived or is precluded by other members of expressing their view on any subject that it is being addressed within the family.

Chapter IVb.
THE KNOWLEDGE OF YOUR PARTNER AND THE TREATMENT BETWEEN THE TWO

The knowledge of the one that is your partner in marriage began in the pre-engagement stage and is a result of that knowledge that you achieved in the stage of courtship and in the final one of marriage.

It is true that in the stages of relating with each other as acquaintances or friends, and dating that not all situations or conditions present themselves in order to learn different facets of the personality of a human being.

Therefore, it is important to know that knowledge of your partner is never complete. It is something dynamic and continuous because we are unique, and we change with age.

Besides, there will always be situations and decisions that we have never faced before.

That is, in this respect, there is no room for routine or monotony.

There will always be details of the personality of your partner that are new to you. Save them in your memory and keep them in mind when making decisions in the future.

Your spouse is unique, unrepeatable, and also has dynamic aspects in his being; learn them; treasure them; use them, and enjoy them.

Trust between partners is also of paramount importance.

You should discuss this aspect because mistrust of one another can be a continual source of problems or misunderstandings between spouses.

Elena and I reached the agreement that we would fully trust in each other.

This decision was based on the following:

-We were married because we loved each other deeply,

-It was a decision for life and was underpinned by honesty in all areas,

-We were both practicing Catholics,

-And rationally, we understood that if you wanted to lie, then it was very difficult that the other could detect it.

Therefore, we concluded that we would trust, one in the other, always and in all areas of our lives.

We would be honest in everything.

So we have done it and maintained it for about 48 years since the beginning of our courtship.

Blessed be God!

Distrust is a constant source of misunderstanding and grievances among couples. Avoid it, please!

If there is any situation about your partner of which you do not know and want to get information, ask outright.

Never stay with the simple desire to know because the mind can take you to draw conclusions and make decisions that can affect your relationship.

When you go to your partner to investigate something, take care of the tone and gestures, etc., as these can interfere in the effectiveness of the dialogue.

Also, depending on the aspect, you must choose the right time to do so.

If the subject that you are addressing is very sensitive to you, then it is good to engage in the dialogue at an appropriate time and place. For example, in a room; just the two of you.

Never try to talk if you are angry or upset with each other.

If one of you loses control and says or does something inappropriate, then it is convenient for the other to apologize and withdraw, or to propose to leave the matter for another time.

But, you should never retire abruptly. This worsens everything.

I recommend that before addressing a subject that is vital for the family, or any of its members, to submit it to the Lord Jesus in prayer.

I assure you, that if you do this and dialogue with all honesty, then you will obtain the Lord's help, and you will strengthen your relationship.

Always treat your partner politely, gently, with courtesy, kindness, and sweetness.

Let him (her) feel your love for him (her) in each of your interactions.

Give him (her) gestures of affection as often as possible: embrace him (her), caress his (her) head, arms, back, etc.

Tell him (her) what he (she) means to you; how important he (she) is to you.

Look for him (her) always; want to be near him (her).

Talk about your love for him (her); do not assume that he (she) knows it and that there is no need to say it.

Even if it was true, and your spouse knows you love him (her), show it to him (her), because it always pleases him (her) that you actually manifest your love.

In my case, for example, every time I'm near Elena, I give her some physical sign of affection.

Also, I express, in writing, various aspects of our relationship and what she represents in my life.
In this way, I consider that she may go back to these expressions of love every time she wants.

For example, one Mother's Day, I wrote, among other things, the following:

"Dear Elena, when I think about mothers, the love God has for us comes to my mind.

It is almost impossible to understand how a human creature, a mere mortal like a mother, can hold in her heart, a feeling so pure, so strong, so immutable, like the love she has for her loved ones, especially for their children.

A mother's love is strong, powerful, constant, unchanging; yet, tender and loving.

It is a love that she gives without expecting or asking anything.

A love that she gives equally to the good, the rebellious, and the bad son.

The mother sees no difference between her children to give her love. She just loves them!

Elena, when I review in my mind, the time our Heavenly Father has given us together and relive your role as a mother, I can only admire the fidelity with which you represent what God wanted to communicate to us through mothers.

You are loving, gentle, tender, kind, and protective of each of our children.

Your love can be "seen" in all your actions, in all your gestures, and your words.

Your life, among us, dear Elena, is a true symphony; a mosaic of love, made in our home every day, every moment, and throughout your life, and we hear and contemplate it with grateful hearts.

What a great honor it is for me, having had the

good fortune to see and enjoy your life as a mother!

Thanks Elena, for maintaining very high, the dignity of mothers.

Love you always, Ricardo Lora "

Another time, in a regular day of our lives, I wrote:

"Dear Elena, I asked myself thoughtfully one day, what attracts me about you?

Everything! Your beautiful and shapely figure, your hair covering your face and neck.

Your quiet and tender look. Your shy smile caressing your lips.

The love of your actions every day and every moment.

Your total commitment, full and humble.

The thousand details that show your love.

Your continuous giving, without asking or expecting anything.

Your relationship with our Heavenly Father and the Blessed Virgin Mary.

That... what attracts me to you? Everything my life, everything!

What a great gift to be in your life!

I love you always, Ricardo Lora"

I think it is a good habit to express, in writing, some feelings for your partner that are difficult to say directly to him (her) verbally most of the time.

The more you know your partner, the easier the relationship between the two.

Over time, the more I know Elena, the more I love her.

What a nice companion the Lord gave me! Thank you my God!

Also, thanks to our Heavenly Mother, the Virgin Mary, who has accompanied us along our relationship of more than 48 years.

She is the one who has fueled our knowledge of: her Blessed Son, His Word, of the Holy Mother Church, and of our Heavenly Father.

Each one of us as human beings has positive and negative aspects.

Focus on the positive aspects of your partner. Enjoy them. Tell him (her) about them!

In relation to the ones, which are negative for you, treat them gently and lovingly with your partner. Make an effort to correct them.

But remember that what you perceive as negative about your partner may be just that, your perception.

Perhaps she or he has no such defect or negativity that you attribute to him (her).

Whatever the reality, say it frankly, but with great tenderness and goodwill.

With sweetness, delicacy, tactfulness, and love, everything can be overcome. I tell you from experience!

Mother Teresa said:

"Do small things with great love."

Chapter IVc.
SEXUAL INTIMACY

The book of Genesis, in The Holy Scriptures, gives us the story of creation.

The Heavenly Father created heaven and earth and all it contains, with its incomparable beauty and majesty:

How could we not enjoy the beauty and grandeur of the sky?

How not to give thanks to God for a sunrise or sunset?

For the incomparable beauty of a mountain covered with snow?

Everything created; God saw that it was good. (Gen1, 12)

God created everything with Love and for Love.

But the most admirable is that God made us in His image and likeness, and He gave us power over all living things:

"1 In the beginning, when God created the heavens and the earth, 27God created man in his image; in the divine image he created him; male and female he created them. 28 God blessed them, saying: Be fertile and multiply; fill the earth and subdue it. Have dominion over the fish of the sea, the birds of the air, and all the living things that move on the earth." (Gen1, 27-28)

Being an image of God, every human being is unique and unrepeatable. It was for the same condition that we were created pure and beautiful, inside and out.

They were naked and not ashamed (Gen2, 25) on the contrary, they felt joyful and enjoyed every creature with its particular beauty.

Because of sin, they lost their inner beauty and felt ashamed to be naked. (Gen3, 10)

This means that if we sin, we will then see our spouse with impure eyes, and we cannot appreciate the beauty with which our Heavenly Father created him (her).

While in this condition, we could "use" our partner for our own benefit.

Let us go frequently to the sacrament of confession in order to mitigate our inclination to sin; so, we can enjoy our spouse and see him (her) with the beauty that God sees him (her). The relationship with our spouse will be pure, pleasant, and enjoyable for both as God expects of us.

When spouses give themselves to each other without limits and without selfishness, we talk of the nuptial meaning of the body.

John Paul II, says:

"4. The human body, oriented interiorly by the "sincere gift" of the person, reveals not only its masculinity or femininity on the physical plane, but also reveals *this value and the beauty of exceeding the purely physical dimension* of "sexuality" [2] 2 . This completes, in a sense, the consciousness of the nuptial meaning of the body, linked to masculinity-femininity of man. On the one hand, this meaning indicates a particular ability to express love in which man becomes a gift, on the other, accounts for the profound ability and availability to the "statement of the person", this is literally the ability to live the fact that the other-the woman for the man and the man for the woman is, through the body, someone who wanted the Creator "by itself", is unique and unrepeatable, someone chosen by eternal Love." (GENERAL AUDIENCE, Wednesday, January 16, 1980)

Now, knowing the love of God for every human being, the least each spouse can do is to respect and love with dignity the other for the love of God who is the loving Father of both of them.

The Holy Father, Blessed John Paul II, continues telling us:

"3. We can say that the interior innocence (that is, the right intention) in the gift exchange is a mutual "acceptance" of another, such as to correspond to the essence of the gift, thus creating mutual donation the communion of persons. Therefore, it is "welcome" to another human being and "accept", precisely because in this mutual relationship that speaks the *Genesis* 2, 23-25, male and female become a gift to each other by the truth and the evidence of his own body in its masculinity and femininity. It is, therefore, an "acceptance" or "host" that expresses and holds in mutual nakedness, the meaning of the gift and thus deepens the mutual dignity about him. This dignity corresponds profoundly to the fact that the Creator willed (and continually wills) man, man and woman, "by itself. Innocence "heart" and, therefore, the innocence of experience means moral participation in the eternal and permanent act of the will of God.

The opposite of this "host" or "acceptance" of another human being as a gift would be a deprivation of the gift itself and thus a changing and even reduced the other to "object to myself" (object of lust, of "misappropriation "etc.)." (GENERAL AUDIENCE, Wednesday, February 6, 1980)

For me, the love between spouses is expressed continuously throughout the day, all lifelong through: looks, a gesture, attention, hugs, caresses, words, etc.

But there are times when that feeling is so great, so strong, so intense that it encourages spouses to give themselves to each other fully and completely.

This intimate union of the two is the communion of persons.

God said, "For this reason a man shall leave his father and mother and be joined to his wife, and the two shall become one flesh." (Mt19: 5)

Intimate sexual relationship is not a goal; it is rather a means to achieve a purpose.

When the relationship with the partner is not selfish, it seeks the satisfaction of the other, and not of oneself. But in doing so, this leads to self-satisfaction.

The outpouring of love between spouses should be expressed throughout the day and in different ways.

Thus, the intimate union of the two is the logical consequence of all these expressions of affection. It is the final form of saying "I love you" to your partner.

It is complete total surrender of yourself to the other.

This gesture says, *"I am fully and completely yours. I belong to you completely and so, I surrender to you with all my love."*

The intimate sexual relationship is not to own it; make it mine, or take it, etc. It is rather surrendered; showing physically the love of one to the other in the most complete form.

It is the union of two so that there are no longer two bodies, but one.

It is the total surrender of one to the other. It is the submission of the self, given fully to the other, for the good and the pleasure of the other.

It should not be a selfish relationship that only seeks its own pleasure. One's pleasure, through this intimate relationship, should be a result of the satisfaction we produce to our partner.

In many books, if not in all the ones that I have read on the subject of the intimate sexual relationship between spouses, they talk about the preparation for that special moment.

Most of them suggest putting on soft music, dimming the bedroom lights; that the woman wears a sexy garment that is provocative to the senses of the man.

To the man, they suggest that he prepare a glass of wine for each, etc.

All this seems fine, but it is an appeal to the senses in order to achieve the physical motivation of the other. Therefore, in my view, it is a selfish approach.

Actually, with all this, what you are looking for is the physical satisfaction per se.

That is, the intimate relationship becomes an end not a means.

It's a carnal desire; some go to extremes using pornographic films, a book of positions, etc., in order to achieve the purpose of arousing the partner.

There is no the expression of love there, of one for the other.

When, however, we seek an intimate relationship to show love totally and completely of one to the other, then we can speak of sex as having an end in itself.

For me, the "preparation" is done throughout the day; all the days of our lives.

Between the couple, if there is a relationship of love and respect, and that love is demonstrated through gestures, actions, and pleasant words, then the intimate relationship arises naturally as a means to express love in a full way, as explained above.

In my case, I say to my wife, more than ten times a day, that I love her.

Every time we are close, I give her some sign of affection: a hug, I kiss her head or cheek, I caress her head, I give her a foot, leg, or back massage, etc.

Each time she does something for me, for example, like giving me some coffee, I thank her and caress her hands or arms.

Elena also does similar things.

She, for example, hugs me from behind, when I'm sitting, caressing my shoulders she sticks her cheek to mine and whispers in my ear, "I love you."

She brings me a glass of water or juice and says, "I brought you water because you have some time here and have not taken anything."

These are tangible ways of showing her love for me.

This is what I call love in action.

Now if all day, the relationship between spouses is distant or if it is not enjoyable. If no affectionate words are exchanged between them, but instead they offend or insult each other, then it is logical that they may not have a desire to have an intimate relationship.

In situations like these, one of the spouses, usually the husband, may use all these means of seduction: music, wine, lighting up candles, etc.; to possess his partner.

This is what I call animalistic -physical union because it appeals only to the senses in the interest of satisfying a biological need for sex.
This is not, therefore, a way of expressing love for each other.

Other authors speak of love play preceding intercourse.

Almost all of them claim to be valid all kinds of caresses and actions between spouses which include kissing genitals and even anal penetration, provided that ejaculation occurs within the female vagina.

Those who suggest these types of caresses justify themselves accordingly because the Church has not condemned it.

I am in total DISAGREEMENT with those who say so.

Oral caresses of the genitals and anal penetration are manipulations of one spouse to the other. It is a selfish act and purely focused on the sexual physical act.

It is not the manifestation of one's love for the other, which is a characteristic that must be present in any intimate relationship between spouses.

Moreover, these two types of "foreplay" damage the pure and holy relationship of conjugal intercourse.

Perhaps the Church has not said anything directly about such actions. But all her teachings, the Holy Scriptures, the writings of the popes, emphasize for us the dignity of the human person.

For example, one of the most important legacies of John Paul II to the Universal Church was the explanation of the relationship between man and woman. Their communion, the communion of persons, through which men and women experience the presence and action of God in their lives.

It is important, to become familiar with the Theology of the Body, that great gift given to us by our remembered and dear Holy Father, the now Blessed John Paul II.

The Theology of the Body designates the content of the 129 Catechesis on Human Love presented by the Holy Father during the public audiences held on Wednesdays from 1979 to 1984.

These moments of intimacy between spouses should be imbued with the purity and dignity with which God created man and woman.

Let us remember what God's Word tells us:

"26Let us make man in our image, after our likeness ...27God created man in his image; in the divine image he created him; male and female he created them." (Gen1, 26-27)

The man and woman are like God in his solitude, says John Paul II, but this similarity is, in all its reality, in the communion of persons: here the spouses become partners of God, if they are open to life. (General Audience of November 14,1979, #s 3 and 4).

The conjugal relationship between spouses should be modeled on the spousal love of Christ the Bridegroom and the Church the Bride. This must be the foundation of all Catholic marriage.

Jesus gave Himself to the church, His wife, with his whole being: body, soul and divinity. When spouses give themselves to each other, in this way, they perform the most noble and sublime act they can do.

Surrendered totally, healthy, holy, selfless, and only for the good of the other. They are imitating the donation that Christ made to His bride, the church at the Cross, and which He continues doing in the Eucharist until the end of time.

John Paul II, says to us with the clarity and depth that is usual to him,

"The virtue of conjugal chastity, and still more the gift of respect for what comes from God, mold the couple's spirituality *to the purpose of protecting the particular dignity of this act.*

The obstacle to this freedom is presented by the *interior constriction of concupiscence,* directed to the other "I" as an object of pleasure. Respect for what God creates gives freedom from this constriction. It frees from all that reduces the other "I" to a mere object and it strengthens the interior freedom of the gift.

This can happen only through a profound appreciation of the personal dignity of both the feminine "I" and the masculine "I" in their shared life. This spiritual appreciation is the fundamental fruit of the gift of the Spirit, which urges the person to respect the work of

God" (General Audience, November 21, 1984, #s 2, 3 and 4)

After reading and understanding the purity and dignity of the human body by design of the Creator and the explanation given to us by the Holy Father John Paul II, we can only wonder of the love our Heavenly Father has loved us with from the beginning.

But there's more, St. Paul, knowing how **stubborn** we are, and perhaps, remembering that Jesus told the Pharisees:

"Moses permitted you to divorce your wife because of **the hardness** of your hearts" (Mt19, 3-9).

And, knowing the Apostle, we always look for an excuse to satisfy our desires, says firmly:

"**16 Do you not know that you are God's temple and that the Spirit of God dwells in you?** 17 If anyone destroys God's temple, God will destroy him. **For God's temple is sacred, and you are that temple**." (ICor3, 16-17)

And the Apostle adds in his letter to the Thessalonians so as to leave no doubt:

"1 Finally, brothers, we earnestly ask and exhort you in the Lord Jesus that, as you received from us how you should conduct yourselves to please

God - and as you are conducting yourselves - you do so even more.2 For you know what instructions ¹ we gave you through the Lord Jesus. 3 ² **This is the will of God, your holiness**: that you refrain from immorality, 4 **that each of you know how to acquire a wife for himself in holiness and honor, 5 not in lustful passion as do the Gentiles who do not know God**; 6 not to take advantage of or exploit a brother in this matter, for the Lord is an avenger in all these things, as we told you before and solemnly affirmed. 7 **For God did not call us to impurity but to holiness**. 8 Therefore, whoever disregards this, disregards not a human being but God, who (also) gives his Holy Spirit to you."(1Tes4, 1-8)

After reading and meditating all these expressions do you still believe that the church must specify what not to do in each case?

For us, everything is very clear!

But I want to introduce an analogy merely appealing to a human reasoning.

Suppose a father tells his children: "Be very careful in the house, your mother and I have bought a very fine crystal glass, very pretty, but very fragile."

One day one of the children walked too close to the crystal with a glass in hand and this made contact with the crystal. A very nice sound was then produced. The young man began to slowly beat the crystal with the glass, wanting to hear the pleasant sound again. He did it several times and the crystal broke.

Was this child's behavior appropriate?

If we reason, similarly to those theologians, justifying the oral-genital and anal games because the Church has not said otherwise, then we may conclude that the child that hit the glass was behaving appropriately.

No dear friends! We know that the conduct of this young man was wrong.

Everyone would get to this conclusion if we fully understood what his dad wanted to communicate when he told his children: the crystal we bought is very pretty and fragile, beware!

Did the parent have to explain to the children all that they could not do to the crystal? Of course not!

By similar reasoning, it is illogical to think that because the Church did not say explicitly that these types of caresses, as love play, should not be practiced that we are then free to perform them.

She, the Church, has called us to holiness, purity, and the dignity of the human body as it were passed to us by Blessed John Paul II and the Apostle Paul.

Remember when Jesus, after explaining a parable, said: "43 He who has ears should listen!" (Mt13, 43)

That is, Jesus himself, after explaining something, felt that what had been said was enough for listeners to understand how to proceed in the future based on the signs given.

"God has assigned as a duty to every man, every woman's dignity." JPII

May the Lord enlighten you with His Holy Spirit!

On the other hand, it is also important to maintain adequate physical care of the body.

For example, when my wife met me, I was a very active person. I practiced several sports: baseball, racket ball, swimming and boxing. In addition, I exercised with weights.

In other words, my body was physically well proportioned.

I have tried to keep my body in similar conditions as which I had when my wife saw me the first time.

Also, personal hygiene is of utmost importance.

It should be noted that the full grooming of the body of both spouses is a delicacy to each other before the intimate relationship.

When you were trying to get the attention of the one, which is now your partner, you certainly cleaned and dressed in a special way for her (him). But now, you must do so more.

She (he) just wants to be flattered by you and only you. He or she deserves it.

Remember, "She (he) is your partner for life." Do not ever forget.

Furthermore, the Scriptures tell us that the husband's body belongs to the wife and the wife's belongs to the husband. (1Cor7, 4)

It is therefore necessary that we carefully care for our body, which belongs to our spouse and the Lord.

Let us get those looks and smiles of satisfaction and joy when our partner looks at us.

All that we have is a gift from God; so, when we perform any activities thank Him for it.

The Book of Tobit tells us that the night that

Sarah and Tobias joined, they prayed to the Lord and He gave them his blessing.

"4 Tobias got out of bed and told Sara, "Arise, sister, and pray to ask the Lord to manifest his mercy and salvation."5 She got up, and both were praying for salvation. He began thus: "Blessed are you, God of our fathers, and blessed be thy name for ever and ever! Let the heavens bless you and all your creatures forever! 6 You made Adam and made Eve, his wife, for your assistance and support, and of these two the human race was born. You said: "No man should be alone. Let a helper fit for him. "7 I am now taking to wife the sister, not to satisfy a passion, but to be a real marriage. Have mercy on her and me, and grant us get together with old age! ". 8 They said: "Amen, amen!" (Tobias 8, 4-8)

I recommend that before having intimate relations that you offer it and pray to God, asking Him at the same time to give you the grace of not offending Him while you manifest the love for each other in this way.

Chapter IVd.
THE TEMPTATIONS

No matter what you do to prevent it, temptations will come.

The enemy, Satan, will not remain inert. He will attempt to make you fall.

Just as our Lord is doing everything possible to help us always to make the right choice every time we make a decision, the enemy, Satan, will try to bring us down the wrong path.

Do not think that you will be free from temptations because you're going to Mass every day, or because you practice the other sacraments, etc. No, the devil will haunt you all your life.

So we should stay away from temptations.

Remember how Satan confused Eve in Paradise.

In the book of Genesis, we find this passage, on temptation and sin of man:

"1 Now the serpent was more subtle than any beast of the field which the Lord God had made, and said to the woman, "Did God ordered them not to eat from any tree in the garden? '. 2 The woman answered, "We may eat the fruit of every tree of the garden.3 But as the tree which is in the middle of the garden, God has said, "Do not eat it or touch it, otherwise you will be subject to death."

4 The serpent said to the woman: "No, not die.5 For God knows that when you eat of the tree to open your eyes and be as gods, knowing good and evil ". 6 When the woman saw that the tree was good for food and pleasing to the eye and desirable for gaining insight, she took of its fruit and ate, then gave it to her husband, who was with her, and he ate.7 Then they opened the eyes of the two and discovered they were naked." (Gen3, 1-7)

Do not overestimate our forces. It is very true when it is say the flesh is weak:

"41 Be warned and pray not to fall into temptation, because the spirit is willing but the flesh is weak." (Mt26, 41)

So, if you see yourself in a dangerous situation to commit any sinful act, get far from it! FLEE! That is what it means to be wise and brave.

The devil dared to tempt even Jesus (Lk4, 1-13). As he, the devil, could not make Him sin, God's Word says:

"13 After exhausting all forms of temptation, the devil departed from him **until the right time**." (Lk4, 13)

That is, the devil never leaves its purpose to make us fall into sin.

I want to include in this part some tips from St. Paul when he addressed the Ephesians and all Christian people:

"10 Finally, be strong in the Lord with the strength of his power.11 Put on the armor of God, to withstand the wiles of the devil.12 For we wrestle not against flesh and blood enemies, but against the principalities and powers, against the ruler of this dark world and against evil spirits inhabiting the space.13 Therefore, take the armor of God so they can withstand in the evil day, and stand firm after having overcome all obstacles. 14 Stand fast, girded with the belt of truth and justice as wearing armor.15 Your feet trace their zeal to spread the Good News of peace.16 Be always on the shield of faith, with which they can extinguish all the flaming arrows of the evil one.17 Take the helmet of salvation and the sword of the Spirit, which is the Word of God." (Ef6, 10-17)

Reading them, we realize that they are meant for us too.

St. Paul, through these words, is emphasizing

to us the importance of prayer. Reminding us in this way that our forces are not enough to cope with the attacks of the devil and his people.

To illustrate, we must not forget in any circumstance that the enemy is always looking for the right time for us to fall into its trap. I will relate one of the many situations that I had to live directly.

I had the opportunity to work in what was, at that time, the largest financial group in the Dominican Republic.

I had a high position in the Bank of that group.

There is a belief, and it seems to be true, that in very prestigious restaurants and bars there are opportunities to do business since many corporate executives tend to visit those places.

Therefore, it was the custom of managers and corporate executives from my bank to go to these places after work.

But in those places there are a lot of social activities and alcohol consumption.

Bank officials used to invite me and when I refused they would say, "You are dominated by your wife."

To which I would reply, "The reality is that my

wife is waiting for me and I have a great desire to see her."

Avoiding places of possible temptations is not for cowards; on the contrary, it is for very brave men and women.

It is also important to keep clear in mind not to be intimate with anyone other than your wife or husband.

We must raise awareness of how weak human nature is and how clever and cunning the enemy of our soul is.

To avoid duplicating information, please review the issues of chastity in Chapter I.

St. Augustine tells each one of us these words:

"This is the battle you have to hold: a continuing struggle against the flesh, the devil and the world.

But fear not, because he who commands us to fight is not an indifferent spectator, nor has he told you to trust only in your own strength."
St. Agustin (Sermon 344.1)

Chapter IVe.
THE HOME ENVIROMENT AND ITS INFLUENCE IN THE DEVELOPMENT AND PERSONALITY OF CHILDREN

During courtship, Elena and I discussed much about our future home.

We addressed all the areas that comprised it.

One area, perhaps the most important, concerned the arrival of the children with whom the Lord would bless our union.

We even thought that four children would be an appropriate number that would allow us to create the ideal conditions to achieve a healthy and integral development of the whole family: especially, the children.

We had a clear conscience of the effect of the home environment on the healthy, balanced, and happy development of the children.

In addition, we knew the role of family in the creation of a good society and a better world for all.

At the 11 month of our marriage, the Lord blessed the house that Elena and I had formed: our first child was born, a beautiful and healthy child, Manuel.

Happiness flooded our bodies in a new and total way. We were parents!

What a beautiful and tender feeling we felt for that creature whom the Lord had entrusted to our care!

As the days passed, our love for Manuel grew as did the feeling of joy of having him with us, but we also realized the great responsibility we had for him.

It was necessary to feed, clean up, and care for him. But we knew that we should do all that with much love and tenderness so that Manuel could perceive it. Thus, he would feel loved and protected.

Furthermore, we ensured that there were no loud noises inside the apartment. Even when speaking, we did it in a tone of voice that would not frighten him.

Remember, it was our first child and we were learning to be parents.

Manuel was born in North Carolina, United States, where I was doing postgraduate studies having been sent by the Pontificia Universidad Catolica Madre y Maestra.

His birth occurred in November, some three months after the initiation of studies in North Carolina University, at Chapel Hill, NC.

Elena did not speak English, and I had great difficulty with the accent of southerners to whom I was listening for the first time.

Moreover, in the area where we lived, there were only a couple of Puerto Ricans who spoke Spanish.

Actually, I think, around Chapel Hill, the hometown of Manuel, no one spoke Spanish. At least, we did not find anyone else in the first few months in that city.

By this I want to tell you that Elena and I had to learn to live alone our new status as parents. No grandparents, no siblings, etc., that might have helped in those first months.

No one related to us assisted us in this most crucial moment for the life of a new couple.

Elena, barely 20 years old, had the responsibility of mother and wife.

I spent the daytime in college while she took care of everything at home.

God and the Blessed Virgin Mary helped her greatly as she completed those labors to perfection.

We had a home! A real home for Manuel, Elena, and me.

We were doing our part and God was doing His.

Blessed be Jesus and Our Heavenly Mother to whom we pray with great devotion since the beginning of our relationship.

Nine months after Manuel was born, Elena was able to travel with him to Santiago, Dominican Republic. Thus the family of Elena and my family could know and enjoy Manuel for the first time.

I could not accompany them for economic and study reasons.

Since that first experience as parents, we decided to create a pleasant environment for all three of us.

We would never talk loudly; we would neither discuss our differences in front of Manuel or the other children that God would give us.

Also, we decided always to respect the decision one of us took with one of our children.

If we thought the decision, correction, or punishment taken by one of the two was inadequate, then the other would let know of it privately, that is, never in front of the children.

Thus, we tried not to lost authority, as parents before the children.

We would do it with great gentleness and tactfulness always thinking of the wellbeing of the children and the home environment.

The person who had made the decision must do the correction that was required at an appropriate time, pointing out to the child or children what was inappropriate and asking to be excused if necessary.

This approach gave us very good results.

After three years in the U.S., we returned to Santiago, Dominican Republic.

After some time, the Lord sent us our second gift, Jennifer, a beautiful girl.

We had a male and a female. What a great joy!

However, God left us Jennifer only for 9 months.

Elena and I agreed in recognizing that Jennifer is the first of our family to get to heaven. That is, our family has a little angel who prays for us and loves us as her parents and siblings.

Of this experience, I will tell you later.

Look now how our Heavenly Father acts.

Perhaps to compensate for this loss, the Lord sent us a pair of twins: Ivette and Eileen.

How delicate and loving is our God!

Thank you Lord! Thank you our Mother!

They had heard our requests in prayer and decided to grant them.

Finally, we received another gift: Angie! She came to complete the family we had planned during our courtship: Elena, 4 children, and myself.

Blessed be God! Hallelujah!

The atmosphere that exists in the home will affect the personality of all that make up that family. Especially, that of the children.

There are plenty of measures that can be taken to achieve the ideal atmosphere that facilitates the healthy and balanced development children.

I will tell you now, as an example, what we did in our home to achieve it.

Elena and I applied, with much fidelity, what we had planned during courtship and early marriage to make our home nice, tidy, with much love, and respect among all and for each other.

Our main goal was to create an environment that would allow and stimulate in the children a healthy and balanced growth. That would help them to create a personality, an attitude of respect, and solidarity for the other household members, and the society in which they would develop their lives.

This way of acting, Elena and I thought, is what they would take with them to school, work, etc.

To achieve that purpose, among other things, we decided the following:

-Make the environment at home physically comfortable.

Elena and I have taken great care that our home was always comfortable and pleasing to the eye.

To realize this, Elena prepared herself in such a way that I cannot describe easily. It is better to tell you what she did.

During courtship, and after marriage, Elena committed herself to know all the aspects that comprised a home: food, décor, and above all the spiritual and religious life.

She dominated them all to such a degree, that she created for me, our children, and herself, a place, our home so nice that we all wanted to get to our house when we were out.

She learned sewing, took cooking courses: basic, gourmet, and other specialties.

She also took baking courses, ceramics, interior decoration, and gardening.

All that, just for us. She never had to work outside the home thanks to the generosity of our Heavenly Father with our family

I can not emphasize enough how important it was for our family and for the environment that has always existed in our home, the fact that Elena was always there while I was working outside.

What a positive impact it is for the children that one of the parents, mainly the mother, is always at their side. Especially, in the early years of their lives.

I know now it is almost impossible that this situation can occur.

For social and mainly economic reasons, both parents must work outside to complete the family budget.

But if that were possible, that one of the parents could stay at home with the children, I recommend it. At least until the kids start going to school regularly, that is, until the age of 5.

Conversely, if a decision is made that both will work outside, then I suggest you plan it in such a way that one of the two of you is at home when the children are in it.

On the other hand, for their feminine characteristics, women can contribute a lot at work and other environments where they operate.

Because it is very relevant of this possible duality of woman as wife and working mother, I present some ideas expressed by Cardinal Ratzinger, our present Holy Father Benedict XVI:

"13. Among the fundamental values linked to women's actual lives is what has been called a "capacity for the other", women preserve the deep intuition of the goodness in their lives of those actions which elicit life, and contribute to the growth and protection of the other.

In this perspective, one understands the irreplaceable role of women in all aspects of family and social life involving human relationships and caring for others.

It means also that women should be present in the world of work and in the organization of society, and that women should have access to positions of responsibility, which, allow them to inspire the policies of nations and to promote innovative solutions to economic and social problems.

Indeed, a just valuing of the work of women within the family is required. In this way, women who freely desire will be able to devote the totality of their time to the work of the household without being stigmatized by society or penalized financially, while those who wish also to engage in other work may be able to do so with an appropriate work-schedule, and not have to choose between relinquishing their family life or enduring continual stress, with negative consequences for one's own equilibrium and the harmony of the family. As John Paul II has written, "it will redound to the credit of society to make it possible for a mother – without inhibiting her freedom, without psychological or practical discrimination and without penalizing her as compared with other women – to devote herself to taking care of her children and educating them in accordance with their needs, which vary with age".[21] (Congregation for the Doctrine of the Faith, May 31, 2004, Joseph Card. Ratzinger *Prefect)*

In addition, I include these words of John Paul II, in his Letter to Women:

"Thank you, *women who are daughters and women who are sisters!* Into the heart of the family, and then of all society, you bring the richness of your sensitivity, your intuitiveness, your generosity and fidelity.

Thank you, *women who work!* You are present and active in every area of life-social, economic, cultural, artistic and political. In this way you make an indispensable contribution to the growth of a culture which unites reason and feeling, to a model of life ever open to the sense of "mystery", to the establishment of economic and political structures ever more worthy of humanity." *(Vatican, June 29, 1995)*

These ideas and contributions of Cardinal Ratzinger and John Paul II can be very helpful for couples to take the decision most appropriate in their particular cases.

Another aspect we decided upon to create the ideal environment in the home was:

-Teach   the children the   proper   way to interact among us.

We should make that relationship with respect, responsibility, gentleness, courtesy, kindness, goodness, fairness, justice, honesty, solidarity, and above all, with love.

They should learn to apologize and to forgive, when necessary.

We will also teach them how important it is to help each other.

This we explained in words and backed it up with the way we did it with them and between us.

For example, Elena and I treat each other always with love and respect. But we also never quarrel in front of the children; on the contrary, we give each other signs of affection: hugs, kisses on the cheek or head. We say thank you and use affectionate words very often.

-Set rules of conduct and behavior that the children should observe closely.

We have read that consistency in the application

of the rules was vital to achieve the desired purpose through them.

We then decided that the rules should be few, fair, and applicable.

Furthermore, we would explain them, the purpose of each rule, so that they understood and every one could meet them.

Example of a rule:

-Upon returning from school, you should: wash your hands, take off your uniforms, put on clothes to be in the house, put school supplies in its place, and prepare for dinner.

This was a rule we established when the children were in elementary school.

In the Dominican Republic at that time, during the 70's and early 80's, the whole family had lunch all together around 1pm.

If any of the children did not do what was decided, then it was required of them to be done, with tenderness and love, but very firmly.

The consistent application of rules decided for the home is the basis of their success.

As an illustration, I want to exemplify the consistency with the case of Amelia.

Amelia is our second granddaughter.

When she was about 4 years old, her parents bought a house and asked Elena and me to help them with the moving. So we did.

When we arrived at the new house, with the first shipment of household items, Amelia bent over to remove her shoes. Her father said, Amelia, do not remove your shoes and thus enter the house!

The girl looked at him, but continued removing her shoes.

Her dad had to insist much so that Amelia obeys.

The reason for the behavior of Amelia was the following:

In the previous house, they had told her that she could not enter the house with shoes on. Her parents had made her comply with this faithfully for about a year.

Look how the consistency in the implementation of this measure had created in Amelia a habit so ingrained in her mind that it was difficult to change.

Not to make this part of the book very long, I must say that as children grow, there will be new rules and others will disappear.

When the established rules could be applied to us, we respected them too. That is to say, we preached by example.

To illustrate, when our children reached an age such that we could allow them to go out with friends, we set these rules:

-If you want to go out with someone, we should know: who you are going out with, where the activity is, at what time does it start, and at what time is it over.

We, then, will set the time to go back home.

In cases that Elena and I had to go out, we told the children where we were going, and the time we would get back.

-You should never smoke or drink alcohol.

Elena and I never smoked or drank alcohol. This does not mean that we did not take a glass of wine with dinner occasionally.

None of our kids smoke or drink alcohol.

After becoming adults, each and every one of them thanked us for these rules and measures taken at home.

When they had to comply with them, they sometimes protested, but finally understood the purpose and benefit to them of such measures and rules at home.

I will present, now, a sample of what our children told us, in writing, after being adults:

1. Some paragraphs of a letter from Angie to me in 2002.

".... On this parent's day, you who are the best of all, not because you are the one I got, but because your heart is so beautiful, so pure, so clean.

You have taught me so much daddy. Thank you for each value instilled, for each correction, for helping so many people, for loving mommy as you love her. You don't know what a joy I feel, seeing how great is your love for her. Thanks for making her so happy all these years, for caring and loving her.

Thanks dad for loving the Lord, thank you, because I find it not hard to love Him, because I know He must be quite the same as you...

I promise to be a person with qualities like you, have strong values, love and help others as you do, love our family and look after it.

Thanks for being just as you are...

May our Heavenly Father fill your heart and soul of His peace and His joy, and Mother Mary be light and guidance in your walk to holiness..."

2. Letter from Eileen to Elena and me when we reached the 38th year of marriage.

"With all my heart congratulations!

May the Lord Jesus continue to bless and strengthen you in love. And above all that the Lord will continue Glorifying in you as a couple, and rejoicing to see that still there are some of His children inviting Him to walk, inviting Him to be the Center of their lives, the Center of their marriage, the Center of their families.

To you Lord, I thank you for given them, the World's Greatest Treasure that is "You"

And the "additions" coming for having You. As the gift of a true Sacrament, the gift of true love... "

3. Letter of Manuel, on a card on my birthday in 2006.

The card brought these words:

"By the way you filled our family life with laughter and happy times for your warmth and understanding, your care and love, we want you to know, dad, how much we love and appreciate you every day of the year"

"Daddy Congratulations!

What this card says, sums up as you are with us all the time. A wonderful example of what we should imitate as man, husband and father. The truth is daddy, I don't know, which of these three, of the many beautiful and good qualities you have, is the greatest in you. Simply, in all of them you are the maximum. I thank God for you, Mom and my sisters..."

4. Letter from Angie, on my birthday, in 2011.

"God manifests Himself in many ways to get to their children ... sometimes it does it through the air, to caress; the sun, to warm us; the water, to give us life. But God in His love and wisdom, thought it was needed more, His tangible presence here on earth and established the paternity, in order to embrace us when we felt fearful, to tell us to rise, when we no longer had strength, to give love without measures or reservations..

I have no words to tell you how much I love you my father, and to thank my Lord, for giving me a father so kind, so loving and so unconditional.

You have put me, and all who are fortunate enough to know you, a high standard to reach you. I hope someday my children can see me with the pride and admiration, with which I can see you today.

You are the one who have taught me more values in my life, not with words but with deeds. Your love for your wife, Mom, and for each one of us. Your respect for all people, whatever their social status, fills me with such pride..."

The expressions in these communications confirm to us that we should strive to nurture our children of all the rules and values that will be useful for the development in their lives and their relationships with others.

To conclude this section, I wish to relate the experience of one of our daughters, with one of the values that we explain and preach at home.

When Angie, the youngest of our children was

17, she was offered the opportunity to participate in an exchange program, which allowed young students to spend a year in another country, staying at the house of a family.

Angie was assigned a family in Belgium that had 4 children: 2 females and 2 males.

A few days after Angie was in that house, the mother (so they call the lady of the house where they were staying) gave her some pills to take. Angie asked why. She replied, "not to become pregnant."

Angie was very surprised. When she could, she told the lady: "If my mother and father know this, they will force me to return immediately."

Then she explained that in most families, of the Dominican Republic, especially in our home, the girls would keep their virginity until marriage.

In Belgium it was the custom for the young girl that after turning 15 years of age she could bring her "boyfriend" to sleep with her in her own home.

I make this story so that we understand as parents that despite our fears, the values we teach in our home will be assimilated and practiced by the children when the situation arises.

Other values that we cultivate in the home, in deed and words: respect for parents and siblings, respect for others, responsibility for their actions, honesty, integrity, solidarity, politeness, etc.

It is important to stress that the child's personality would be affected positively or negatively depending on reactions of other household members, but especially that of the parents on the behavior of the children.

We should remember that every human being has the need to feel welcomed, accepted, valued, and useful among other things.

Furthermore, what we believe and think of ourselves, in fact, is determined by what we believe others think and believe of us.

That is, self-acceptance depends on other persons and not on myself.

The concept of me is communicated from others when they relate to me.

If I perceive that I am worthy, that I am useful, good, etc.. then that same thing is what I will get to think of myself.

In short, who I am and how I react to others has been determined in my life by the relationships with others.

Therefore, in the relationship with our family, at work, and school, etc., we must be aware of this great reality.

Let us try that our actions and reactions to others help them form a positive self-image of themselves.

If we all do the same, then we will have: good, healthy, happy people, etc.., united, caring, and nice families, etc.. This will result in a society and a world that is more just and happy.

I think this worth any effort we have to do to achieve it. Why not try it now, today?

Never is too late to start, start now!

To your spouse, your children, brothers, dad, mom, etc.., let them know with your behavior, in your relationship with them, that their opinions, their collaboration, help, etc. is loved, accepted, desired, etc.

This will help them feel useful, loved, accepted, desired, etc. for others and self-satisfaction will increase. Their self-esteem will be great and positive.

There is no other most important need for the human being than this, of being accepted and taken into account by others.

If in the family, all create awareness that if we accept and respect the other as he (she) is, then we will be able to increase his (her) self-esteem.

Co-existence will be quite pleasant and fruitful when all household members have a positive self-esteem.

Considering all these factors, parents need to correct, talk, and discuss with their children, with great tactfulness and love; in order to encourage in them those aspects of their personality that will be of great benefit to them as adults.

I wish to emphasize once again that the parents and elders at home must love children unconditionally. That is, our children must see that we just love them.

That our love for them does not depend on what they do or not do, but that we love them as they are.

We should avoid giving gifts, for example, if they get good grades in school, and punishments if they do not.

Actions like these could make the child to believe that to be loved and accepted he must do this or that.

Such actions and reactions could seriously affect the personality of the children.

His conduct as an adult could be marked by these experiences.

It is far better that children perceive the love of the other household members, especially parents, as a love for themselves as individuals.

It is in this way that our Father God loves us. He loves us regardless of our behavior, but as a good Father, He wants us to be better every day.

Another important aspect that families should practice is to share together whenever this is possible.

All effort should be made to share together one meal of the day.

Maybe dinner is the most feasible option in the world today.

Use this moment to give thanks to God for the food and all the blessings we receive from Him as a family every day.

When all household members are at home, isolation from each other should be avoided through the use (abuse) of the cell phone, iPod, TV, or PC.

By contrast, they should look for activities or games that will enable them to share together as a family.

The most important is prayer in common.

The Holy Rosary is a prayer that helps the integration of the whole family in an action shared by all.

It's good that parents teach their children by words and example of how essential it is to practice their Catholic religion: attending Mass every Sunday and religious holidays, making the Sacrament of Penance, confession, at least once a month, participating in activities prepared by the Church for the faithful such as courses and retreats that increase awareness of our religion and reinforce our faith.

Elena and I always accustomed our children to pray together, go to Mass every Sunday and holy days, to know and practice the sacraments, and to thank God for all that He gives us daily, etc.

At the time that our children were growing up, between the years 1970-1994 in the Dominican Republic, it was possible to have lunch together and so we always did.

During lunch, we gave thanks to God and alternated between members so that all could lead that moment of family intimacy and gratitude to our Heavenly Father and the Blessed Virgin.

Another custom, which we developed in our home and still live after more than 40 years was to go out to eat together every Sunday.

That was an inflexible practice. We ate and shared as a family. Then, the children could meet with friends and relatives.

This practice deepened in each one of us so much, that our children, all adults now, still join Elena and me to go out and share lunch provided they are at home or close to it since some of them are already married.

Our children remember that practice with great pleasure.

Elena and I learned to enjoy all the activities that we could share with our children.

For example, we did oversea trips together.

Elena and I never traveled alone. This we only did if I had to travel on business matters. How much joy and confidence developed among family members when sharing like that!

For me, this is because household members get to know each other better when they share those moments of family life in a happy and healthy way. The fact that there were no phones, i-pods, etc., helped in this situation a lot. These latter gadgets separate the family members today.

So, I want to emphasize that when the family is doing a common activity, each one of the members should avoid anything that separate them from the rest of the family, like: privately listening to music, talking on the phone, communicating by text, etc.

You should enjoy the most the moments you can share together.

Elena and I gave such importance to family time together, that we never allowed having a TV, for example, in the rooms.

We considered that this could affect family integration, and we had done everything possible to keep the family strongly united.

I do wish to refer to the following important aspect often neglected as spouses.

After God blesses the home with children, communication between spouses often revolves around issues related to the children.

Over time, this becomes so common that if the spouses do not realize it, they will gradually lose the habit of talking as spouses, and will do so, just as parents.

You need to pay attention to this possibility of losing the relationship as a couple.

We encourage you to seek time to share as husband and wife. Whenever possible: go to movies, to dinner, to dance, etc. That is, do activities that help strengthen the affection and love between the two of you.

You could sometimes also share time with married friends and/or family.

Remember that over time if the Lord our God grants you a long life, it is possible then that you two will be alone again, as you started.

The children will have left from home to form their own families.

If you did not take time to maintain the relationship as a couple, then you run the risk of having nothing to talk about between the two.

You began alone and so, alone you might end. Therefore, keep alive even with the children present the relationship as spouses, friends, and colleagues.

Continually share the expressions of affection, of tenderness, of love, which led the two of you to courtship and then to marriage.

This is worthwhile. I tell you from experience.

Let me conclude this chapter with the exhortations to the families of the Holy Father, Benedict XVI:

"Dear families, be brave! Do not yield to the secular mentality that proposed coexistence as proposed to prepare and even substitute for marriage.

It is well known that the Christian family is a special sign of the presence and love of Christ and that is called to give a specific and irreplaceable contribution to evangelization.

The Christian family has always been the main route of transmission of the faith, and today has great potential for evangelization in many areas. Dear Parents, always strive to teach your children to pray, and pray with them, bring them to the sacraments, especially the Eucharist, place in the life of the Church, do not be afraid to read the Scriptures in private domestic, illuminating Family life with the light of faith and praising God as Father.

Be like a small upper room, like that of Mary and the disciples, in which you live the unity, fellowship, prayer " (Vatican City, June 5 meeting 2011, First National Encounter of Croatas Catholic's Family.SSBenedict the XVI" Christian family. Call to Evangelization.)

Chapter IVf.
OPEN TO LIFE

Although Elena and I had planned that the ideal family for us was composed of 4 children and the two of us, for our condition as Catholics we were open to life.

That is, we would welcome the children that the Lord wanted to give us.

I remind you that Manuel, our first child, was born in the United States when I was studying for the master and doctorate degrees at the University of North Carolina at Chapel Hill, North Carolina.

For a specific condition, every human being has an Rh factor that can be positive (+) or negative (-).

Thus, we speak that I am Rh +, or that Elena is Rh-.

Well, the reality is this: Elena has a negative Rh and I am Rh positive.

We were unaware of that until Elena's first pregnancy.

The doctor attending to Elena at the hospital of the University told us that this difference in Rh between us could have negative consequences for Elena and the child to be born.

Imagine, Elena was 20 years old and I 26. We were in a strange country, United States of America. We were Dominicans. Elena had not learned English and I was in my first semester of studies.

We were alone. No family. No friends.

It was in these circumstances that the Lord sent us Manuel, our first beloved son. Shortly after birth, Elena started to breastfeed Manuel.

Two days after birth, we noticed and so informed the doctor that Manuel's skin was turning yellow.

They began to investigate and did not find what was causing it.

At one point in the process, they informed me in the hospital that I had to sign an authorization for them to give a blood transfusion to Manuel if necessary.

I had no choice so I signed that paper.

In all that time, Elena and I prayed to the Lord and the Blessed Mother without stopping, presenting them the situation we were living.

The prayer worked and the Lord enlightened the doctor who was attending to the child.

He asked Elena to discontinue giving breast milk to Manuel.

After Elena stopped breastfeeding him, the yellow color disappeared from Manuel's skin.

The doctors had then realized that Elena's milk was producing a negative reaction in Manuel.

Thanks to God, this situation was overcome!

The doctor explained to us that after each birth, Elena would have to get an injection in order to avoid problems in future pregnancies. This was done.

After returning to the Dominican Republic, Elena became pregnant a second time and our first daughter, Jennifer, was born.

We had a young couple: male and female.

We went through the same process and Elena was injected again.

I want to clarify that because of what happened to Manuel with Elena's breast milk, we decided that she would not nurse any other children because of the potential danger that existed.

Everything was going well and we were very happy, but Jennifer got sick and the Lord decided to take her back to her heavenly home when she was 9 months old.

Elena and I agree that Jennifer is the first of our family to go to Heaven. We have an angel who cares for us!

That's true, but the suffering from losing a child is so great that it is impossible to describe; especially, when it happens at such a young age.

Our faith and constant prayer was, and is, the only thing that has allowed us to live with that reality.

Inevitably, I associated the loss of Jennifer with Elena's being Rh negative and me being Rh positive.

I also thought that what had happened to Manuel, shortly after being born, was due to the same Rh factor differences between us.

I had a little fear that our future children could be in danger too.

The loss of our beloved daughter directed us even more to prayer.

Elena and I prayed continuously, asking the Lord to sustain us in this period so difficult in our lives.

Some time after the death of Jennifer, we decided to put the decision of having more children into the hands of our God and the Blessed Virgin so that they would decide if they were going to give us any more children.

The Lord and the Blessed Mother heard our prayers and petitions and to take away the doubts and fears sent us twins: Ivette Marie and Eileen Marie.

How great and generous is the Lord!

How good is our Blessed Mother!

The doctor reminded us again that Elena should not continue having children because of the danger to her and the child (ren) represented by the differences of Rh between the two of us.

Despite these suggestions, of Elena's attending physician, we continued looking for more children.

Finally, the Lord sent us Angie.

We had four children as we had planned!

When Angie was born, I was concerned for her life due to Elena's Rh factor.

This story of the birth of our children and the fact that Elena is Rh negative and that I am Rh positive, has as the main reason our desire to explain the great mistake that Elena and I made out of ignorance.

We want to highlight this error so that none of you commit it.

Chapter IVg.
THE BIG MISTAKE

After Angie's birth, the Dr. attending to Elena during pregnancy and childbirth said emphatically, referring to Elena:

"You definitely should not continue having children. The risk is very great for your life and for the life of the child."

The doctor suggested to Elena a number of ways of how not get pregnant.

One of them was to operate her so she could not have more children.

Elena has always had much fear of operations. We therefore decided, and I accepted, that they perform a vasectomy on me.

This was in 1975.

Anyone would think that medicine was too far behind because it did not have a solution for the case of Rh negative mothers, with Rh positive parents.

In deciding to write this, I inquired what the medicine of 2011 was saying.

I found an article on the internet, which referred to this issue.

To my surprise I found the following, I will present only just some of the ideas.

If the mother is Rh negative and the expected baby is Rh positive like the baby's father, then the mother's immune system which fights the invaders to keep her healthy, will recognize the red blood cells of the baby as foreign to the mother's Rh negative blood. Thus, the mother will begin producing antibodies to destroy the baby's red blood cells.

Once these antibodies start attacking, they can decrease the baby's red blood cell count, which can lead to jaundice, anemia, mental retardation, and/or heart failure.

In severe cases, it can also be fatal to the womb (during pregnancy), or shortly after birth.

All this would bring consequences, serious complications that could endanger the life of her children, and that would be very difficult to try and resolve.

After 36 years, and if we take the year Manuel was born, 1967, that is 44 years later, medicine was still saying the same thing that they told us back then.

On the other hand, and due to ignorance on our part of the guidelines of the Catholic Church in regard to the methods of preventing children, we made this mistake.

I will explain what we did, not as a justification, but for you to avoid and help others also not to make the mistake that we made, in this case.

Although Elena and I came from practicing Catholic families, we were unaware of the regulations of the Church about Natural Family Planning.

For us, being open to life meant not to abort, but it was not a sin that Elena avoided pregnancy in any way whatsoever.

In the years when we got married, the mid-1960's, parents did not talk about sex with their children. Thus, neither Elena nor I received information on this sensitive topic.

The Lord knows that we are telling the truth and He will judge us according to His mercy.

When we found out how wrong we had been, we confessed this sin.

We also got information about what the Catholic Church allowed or approved as methods for Family Planning like the Rhythm Method and the Symptothermal Method.

We strongly recommend that all couples become familiar with these methods before marriage.

If you are married, you must also learn about these methods and choose the one most appropriate to your reality.

"The way to plan the Family is Natural Family Planning, not contraception. In destroying the power of giving life, through contraception, a husband or wife is doing something to self. This turns the attention to self and so destroys the gift of love in him or her. In loving, the husband and wife must turn the attention to each other. Once that living love is destroyed by contraception, abortion follows very easily" (Mother Teresa)

Months after I learned of our mistake and knew the methods accepted by our Holy Mother Church, I then asked my mother: Mom, what method did you and dad use for family planning?

My mom looked at me mischievously with a big smile and said, "Your dad wanted me to use, what ever was necessary to avoid getting pregnant. Since, he said, 'We had many children'. To which I would reply, the only thing I'm willing to do not to get pregnant is this, whenever you enter the room, I leave it. Nothing else!"

At that time, I laughed at the response and decision of my mother.

But, analyzing it now, I realize that "my mother's method" for family planning is fully open to life and safer in accomplishing its goal.

My mom's method is the one I like the most, what about you?

I recommend it whole heartedly.

Chapter IVh.
MONEY AND THE FAMILY

Money has become the ideal instrument for the exchange of goods and services. It is therefore a means to an end; not an end in itself.

We should have this aspect very clear because society has given great power to people who have a lot of money.

As a result, a lot of people make and are willing to do whatever it takes to get and hoard money; be these actions legal or not, moral or not.

The way does not matter. What counts is the result some would say.

Jesus says:

"19 Do not store up treasures on earth, ..., 20 Accumulate, however, treasures in heaven, ..., 21 For where your treasure is, will your heart" (Mt6, 19-21).

We must avoid having our hearts clung to money.

It is true that it is necessary, but only God is indispensable. Therefore, in our hearts God must be at the center. The rest, He will give to us as the good Father He is.

Other persons might even say, "I'll get money. Whatever the cost."

A mentality like this was perhaps what led Judas Iscariot to betray and deliver Jesus for thirty pieces of silver:

"14Then one of the Twelve, who was called Judas Iscariot, [7] went to the chief priests15[8] and said, "What are you willing to give me if I hand him over to you?" They paid him thirty pieces of silver."(Mt26, 14-15).

Many people accumulate money and make money their "god"; they believe that in today's society, you can get everything with money.

Caution! It is true that money is necessary to meet our needs, but we should get it honestly with our work and never make it our "god"!

Love for another "god" that is not our Heavenly Father, Jesus, or the Trinity, but for money, power, and recognition, etc.., will take one and society to moral ruin and perdition.

This is what is currently happening in the world for having departed from God and removing him from virtually all areas of our lives and relationships with others.

If we do not return to God and His commandments to center our lives, then the progress of science and technology will have served for nothing. We will inevitably walk towards total destruction.

We still have time. Let's put God at the center and see how everything will be different and better!

Jesus warns us so that we do not put money as the most important thing in our lives when he says:

"24 No man can serve two masters, either he will hate one and love the other, or be interested in the first and despise the second. You can not serve God and money." (Mt6, 24)

He also stated: "25 Yes, it is easier for a camel to go through the eye of a needle than a rich man to enter the kingdom of God." (Lk18, 18-27).

In this expression, the Lord means that money must be used for what it is, a means to facilitate the exchange of goods and services and also to help others meet their needs.

When we do it this way, whether we are rich or poor, we will be walking along the road that leads to eternal life.

In marriage and family, we need money to cover household expenses like housing, food, health, education, etc... and also for charity.

At home, we teach the children by words and deeds of the appropriate way to use money that enters the home.

Explaining to them that the family must live according to their income level.

This must determine the type of home you buy, the car, its social activities, vacations, etc.

Emphasize to the children that we should neither be guided by consumer advertising, nor by the pattern of society.

These, with few exceptions, want to motivate us to consume improperly: for fashion, for competition, for the imitation and the consumption of others, etc.

The Word of God, the Bible, teaches us to live modestly and to help others who do not have sufficient resources to meet their needs.

That is, we must practice love of neighbor.

Emphasize in these explanations that all you have is by God's grace; therefore, we owe thanks to Him and His Church.

Jesus addressed the issue of money thousands of times.

From His teachings, we can conclude that money itself is not bad, but that our use of it is or may be bad.

"3 Blessed are the poor in spirit, for theirs is the kingdom of heaven" (Mt5, 3).

That is, the Kingdom of God comes to us with Jesus and to our lives when we accept Him.

Only the poor in spirit, the humble, those who are not blinded by material wealth, can accept and live the teachings of Jesus.

Charity, that is, the help we can offer to people and/or institutions to fill or cover their personal and/or social needs are stimulated by the Holy Mother Church.

Our Holy Catholic Church depends on each and every one of those who compose it; of all of its faithful in order to meet its needs and for the social aid she also does around the world.

Despite the importance of the contribution to the Church, Jesus reminds us how essential the relationship with other human beings is when He presents to us the following situation:

"22 But I say that whoever is angry with his brother, deserves to be condemned by a court. And anyone who insults him deserves to be punished by the Sanhedrin. And he who curses him, deserves the Gehenna of fire.23 Therefore, if you are offering your gift at the altar and there remember that your brother has something against you, 24 leave your gift before the altar, go and be reconciled to thy brother, and then come and offer your gift." (Mt5, 22-24)

The contribution to the Church is related to the amount of money we have and/or make with our work.

It is important that the contribution to the Church be part of our budget, and not something we take of our surplus.

Jesus, looking at the people giving alms in the temple, saw a poor widow giving a few coins, and told his disciples:

"I assure you that this poor widow has given more than anyone.4 For everyone else did as offering some of their wealth, but she out of her poverty, gave all she had to live."(Lk21, 1-4)

Therefore, our contribution to the Church, and the help for charities, must have as an essential and common element, the love with which we do it.

St. Paul, in one of his letters, tells us that we can do anything, but do not have love, we gain nothing. (1Cor13, 1-3)

I will now tell you two anecdotes relating to:

1) Our experience giving the contribution to the Church, and

2) Practicing charity with the poor.

First anecdote: Making our contribution to the church.

In the Catholic Church in the Dominican Republic, the faithful contribute freely the amount of money they want every Sunday when the offertory collection is performed. Generally, it is done in cash by placing the donation within the basket that it is passed by for this purpose.

Elena and I contributed with a fixed amount every Sunday.

From time to time, we increased that amount, and we kept it for several months. We then increased the donated amount again.

Over time, I noticed something that caught my attention: the amount of money that we received at home had been increasing continuously from time to time.

I told Elena that I noticed that the greater our contribution to the Church, the greater the amount of money that we receive.

How great is our God! He does not allow himself to be outdone in generosity.

Second anecdote: The practice of charity.

Elena and I attended Mass at the House of the Annunciation in Santo Domingo.

Several people often stood in front of the church there to ask for alms from those who came.

One of them, a lady, was never satisfied with the money I gave her.

If there were five people, then I would give each one of them the same amount. They all would say, "Thanks, God bless you," except her.

Conversely, without looking at what had been given to her, she asked to be given more.

On several occasions, I attended to her petition and gave her more.

This was repeated for several weeks. I noticed that even giving her up to three times more than I did to the others that this lady wanted even more.

This attitude came to bother me so much that I even thought to go to another church in order to partake of the Holy Eucharist.

One day, before the Blessed Sacrament in the Adoration Chapel, I told the Lord:

"Holy Father, I'm tired of this lady's attitude, even though I am giving her much more than the others, she is never satisfied. I have thought to stop coming here so as not to meet her."

Having just said that, the Lord put the following in my mind: "Would you like that I do the same with you?"

I felt totally embarrassed because I realized all that I continually asked of God and how He has never rejected me.

I decided to give the lady the same amount I was giving the others and so I informed her.

Let's see now some parables that Jesus told his disciples and so understand the rightful place of money in our lives.

First Parable. In which He presents them the case of a farmer who had a great harvest and said to himself: I will build a large barn, will store my harvest and I will give myself a great life.

But God said, "Fool, this very night you will die. And who will own what you have amassed?"(Lk12, 116-21)

With this new parable Jesus wants us to remember that although material possessions are needed, what is most important, and we should never forget, is to be prepared for eternal life, because we do not know when we will get the call to report ourselves to the House of our Heavenly Father.

Second Parable. Of the sower. Here I will talk only of the seeds that fall among thorns, and the thorns grew up and choked it.

Jesus says, "it happen the same to the one, which blinded by wealth, does not endorse the Word and implement it in its life, but obsessed and attached to wealth, does not bear fruit. That is, does not do any charity work.

Instead, he lives enslaved of what society preaches, would give him freedom and absolute control of his lives and its environment, the money." (Mt13, 3-23)

We know that it's not like society tells us. Therefore, our faith, our lives, and our family are centered in God.

We follow this way, the mandate of the Gospel:

"You shall love the Lord, your God, with all your heart, with all your being, with all your strength, and with all your mind" (Lk10, 25-27)

Jesus adds: "But seek first the kingdom (of God) and his righteousness, [19] and all these things will be given you besides." (Mt6, 33)

Usually, as a result of learning and of society, we have become planning creatures.

We want to have control of all of the aspects of our lives in all circumstances, and that's not bad. But, we lose control of many areas because of selfishness, envy, and/or inadequate competences, etc.

To show the effects it can have on our budget and our family when we follow the teaching of society and the world, we will illustrate with some examples:

1. We have planned our expenses in relation to our income, but the neighbor, friend, or coworker, bought a Mercedes.

I do not want to be left behind and also bought a similar car, or a more expensive one.

My income, however, was not enough to buy that type of vehicle, and so my budget is going down and eventually collapses.

2. The same happens with the house we buy for our family.

For that same desire, to have a house "better" than my friend or acquaintance, I buy a house, which is far above, my economic possibilities and so the family budget is destroyed.

3. Something similar happens with the social life we lead: It is well above our means. Result: budget imbalance.

When we act in the manner described above, we generally have to cut activities, areas, etc. perhaps, those of much priority than the investments made.

This creates tension, arguments, and actions that seriously affect the relationship between the spouses, children, and all that composes this home.

I remember that while working in a financial group, there were many executives that were earning less than I, but wanted to live a standard of living for reasons of social competence well above their income.

As a result, they had to be borrowing or asking advancements of their potential annual bonus.

Such behavior caused some of them even to lose their homes and cars.

In the case of Elena and me from the beginning, we decided to live below our level of income.

The Lord always helped us to have sufficient income to cover all the needs of the family.

To date, 45 years of marriage, we have never lacked anything necessary in our home.

Blessed be our Heavenly Father!

Let us not allow ourselves to be dragged by consumerist advertisements, neither by envy, or ostentation.

Remember and make it your own, what Jesus told his disciples and followers, "You are in the world but are not of the world" (Jn17, 16)

Telling us with this that we should not follow the guidelines of society, but the guidelines that He left us in the Scriptures and that which the Holy Mother Church teaches us to practice.

It is important to remember, that money can be an element of division in the home and especially between spouses.

If one of them, for example, wants to control the use made of the money they have in a manner that is especially authoritarian and gives no participation, no freedom to the other to also make use of it, then it can produce a situation such that it affects all aspects of the marriage relationship.

The same can happen if each has a separate account of the monetary resources they have.

To me, this latter situation of separate accounts tells me that, in the mind of at least one of the two, there is the possibility that marriage may end sometime in the future.

If this is your case, review your relationship and strengthen the trust between the two. Put your relationship under the loving care of Jesus and the Blessed Virgin Mary. They can always help.

We now present some practical ideas that have given excellent results to my family:

1) Elena and I have all of our possessions in common: money, house, cars, credit cards, etc.

We've never had anything material in the name of only one of the two.

Of course, we have talked abundantly on the responsibility of its use: how much resource we have available, what are the needs and the priorities of them, etc.

If in doubt, consult with the other.

Being clear about this, we can freely make use of the goods that our God has provided so generously to us in all these years of marriage.

2) In general, live a standard of living, which can be covered with the normal income of the family.

3) Have one or a maximum of two credit cards.

Although credit cards can greatly facilitate payments and make transactions more convenient, it is also true, that it is the money that pays the most interest.

Some credit card issuers are now charging up to 29.99% annual interest.

So you can appreciate how expensive these interest rates charged by credit cards are, I inform you that the banks are paying $ 0.30% annual interest on Certificates of Deposit.

We are saying this in March 2012.

So our rule is to pay the total balance on the credit card monthly on the due date.

Thus, we use the money from the card issuer on average for a month without interest or administrative fees.

4) Maintain relations and social activities at a manageable level with our income.

We know of families that borrow money to go on vacations, or to celebrate the 15 birthday of their daughter.

Some have even mortgaged their house!

No, please! Do not do that ever!

Others relate with friends of a higher level of income, and that's not bad.

We have friends from all social classes.

The problem arises when we want to imitate the standard of living of one of those friends, or when a situation arises, and it is appropriate, to make a gift to the friend who has a lot of money.

Some do it of such a price that it unbalances the family budget.

Ultimately, it is important that your home, your car (s), your jewelries, etc., are in line with your income level.

Enjoy healthfully what the Lord gives you. Do not envy what others have.

There is a saying that people repeated a lot in my youth: "The happiest man on earth had no shirt."

"The less we have, the more we give. It seems impossible, but it is not. That is the logic of love" Mother Teresa.

Money does not purchase happiness. You will get it with the attitude you have towards life and in having your gaze fixed on the ultimate goal: eternal glory.

Jesus says: "Do not work for food that perishes but for the food that endures for eternal life, ¹"(Jn6, 27)

Remember, we are citizens of heaven, and live temporarily in the earth.

"11And now I will no longer be in the world, but they are in the world, while I am coming to you. Holy Father,... 15⁶ I do not ask that you take them out of the world but that you keep them from the evil one.16They do not belong to the world any more than I belong to the world." (Jn17,11.15-16)

Something, which is very true, is that the generosity with which we treat others will be an important factor to the degree of satisfaction that we will have in this life.

God is so good that He gives us the grace to receive greater happiness by doing a work of charity than by the reception of a gift.

I have seen the accuracy of this statement many times throughout my life.

Who should we help? The one needing our help; be it family or not.

The Lord Jesus illustrates this in the parable of the Good Samaritan that we saw earlier.

However, I suggest you read it again. (Lk10, 29-37)

But it is very important to remember that by practicing charity with someone, we should do it with and for love.

Chapter IVi.
FAMILY PRAYER

The most important aspect of the family and for each of those who compose it is the life of prayer.

Prayer is a dialogue between God and man. It is the elevation of the soul to God; therefore, it should be done with great humility.

St. Ambrose tells us that in order for the dialogue to take place, after praying, we must read Scripture: we speak to Him when we pray, hear God when we read His words (CCC # 2653)

Prayer can be of: petition, intercession, thanksgiving, praise, etc. (CCC#s 2629 to 2643)

Everything we've tried so far in this book is helpful for the development of the family, but nothing, nothing can replace prayer, this necessary, useful, and enjoyable relationship of all and every one with God.

The success, harmony, peace and satisfaction at home will be directly linked to the life of prayer of the whole family and each individual of that home.

Our home has worked very successfully from the beginning.

Elena and I attribute this to the constant family and individual prayer life we have always lived.

We believe that if we built our house, our home, and our lives on the rock that is Jesus, then we have the absolute guarantee that we will be successful in every area of our existence.

"24 Thus, everyone who hears the words I say and put them into practice can be likened to a wise man who built his house upon a rock.25 The rain came down, rushed the torrents, the winds blew and shook the house, but this did not collapse because it was built on rock.26 On the contrary, he who hears my words and does not practice, can be likened unto a foolish man who built his house on sand. 27 The rain came down, rushed the torrents, the winds blew and shook the house, and it fell and great was the fall." (Mt7, 24- 27)

In these verses from the Gospel of Matthew, Jesus tells us what it means to build on rock; namely, to listen to His words, His teachings, and implement them.

It is, fundamentally, to believe in Jesus and believe Him. In other words, it is to love Him and live according to His teachings and mandates.

"If you love me, you will keep my commandments. Whoever has my commandments and observes them is the one who loves me. And whoever loves me will be loved by my Father, and I will love him and reveal myself to him." (Jn14, 15-21)

"5 I am the vine, ye are the branches He who abides in Me and I in him, bears much fruit, for apart from me you can do nothing.

7 If you remain in me and my words remain in you, ask whatever you want and get it. 8 The glory of my Father is that you bear much fruit, and so are my disciples.9 As the Father has loved me, so have I loved you. Remain in my love.10 If you keep my commandments, you remain in my love. As I have kept my Father's commandments and abide in his love." (Jn15, 5. 7- 10)

Only if we obey the commandments of Jesus, abiding in His love, will we be building our lives in Him.

And so, what are those commandments?

They are contained in all Scripture; especially, in the New Testament.

As an illustration, we will refer to some of them.

a) "Love your neighbor as yourself." (Mt22, 39)

And who is our neighbor?

The person who is in need who requires our help.

Jesus illustrated who our neighbor was with the parable of the Good Samaritan. (Lk10, 29-37)

In the mandate to love our neighbor as ourselves, the reference point, or the model used to love another, is ourselves.

After spending time with his disciples and having lived a while with people of His time, Jesus knew that we did not know how to properly love ourselves.

Jesus then changed the model that we must see when we express our love to others. We were not more the model but Jesus himself. So He said:

b) Love one another as I have loved you.

"34 I give you a new commandment: love one another. As I have loved you, love you too each other. 35 By this all will know that you are my disciples, who have love for one another "(Jn13, 34-35)

The reference, of how to measure our love for others, is Jesus. We must love as Jesus loves.

And how did Jesus love us? He loved us with his whole being, even giving his life for us.

c) Work for food that endures and that gives you eternal life.

"27Do not work for food that perishes but for the food that endures for eternal life, [15] which the Son of Man will give you. For on him the Father, God, has set his seal."(Jn6, 27)

True, we must try to satisfy all the material needs of our family, but we must put more interest in achieving that everyone is prepared for eternal life.

This we can achieve with constant prayer, frequent practice of the sacraments: penance (confession), and the Eucharist.

It is important that all family members participate in the sacramental life.

We should note here that all our children received, at the relevant time, the Sacraments of Christian initiation: Baptism, Confirmation, and Eucharist.

It also may serve us, in preparation for eternal life, to practice charity with all of those we can help.

Permanent prayer is good, but if we do not practice what we learn of Jesus, then there will be no consistency between our words and our practical life.

The apostle James shows us very clearly, he tells us:

"7So also faith of itself, if it does not have works, is dead.18Indeed someone might say, "You have faith and I have works." Demonstrate your faith to me without works, and I will demonstrate my faith to you from my works."(James2, 17-18)

d) Talking about our faith, we all say with great conviction: I love God very much.

This may be true, but how do we express to God our love for Him?

A good friend of my family, Chelo, told us that while in prayer she said to Jesus, "I want to show my love for you."

Jesus told her: "If you want to love me, then love a brother. If you want to hug me, then hug a brother.

The only way you can show your love for me

while on earth is through your brothers. There is no other way.

Now you know. Show your love for Jesus, through all persons with whom you relate.
Love them as you would love Jesus!

e) In life, whether in the family or any other human group, we seek to occupy the best positions, the best posts, etc.

That is not how Jesus thinks. He wants to show that "importance" is obtained through unselfish service to others.

On one occasion, the disciples argued about who was the greatest among them.

Jesus took advantage of this to say:

"43 But it shall not be so among you. Rather, whoever wishes to be great among you will be your servant; 44 whoever wishes to be first among you will be the slave of all. 45 For the Son of Man did not come to be served but to serve and to give his life as a ransom for many."(Mk10, 43-45)

In the case of Elena and me, when we say that the success of our family is due to the fact that we build our house, our home, our lives, on the rock that is Jesus, we mean to say that we have tried to live by His teachings.

Prayer has always been present in our family.

Every day we pray the Holy Rosary of the Virgin Mary and the Chaplet of Divine Mercy.

In addition, for about 17 years, we have a prayer group in our home that is open to all who wish to participate. We meet every Friday at 8:30 PM.

How many blessings have been poured out by Jesus and the Blessed Virgin in our home and in the homes of the people who have participated along with us in the prayer of The Holy Rosary!

We read some passages every day from The Holy Bible.

Elena and I partake of the Eucharist daily: The Mass.

And so, we receive the body and blood of Jesus, every day. What a great honor!

We participate, frequently, of the Sacrament of Penance, Confession.

Our grown children are involved as facilitators in groups that offer workshops for people over 18 years of age, about chastity, for couples and married couples.

We practice charity in many ways, but here we follow the advice of Jesus:

"2 When you give alms, do not blow a trumpet before you, as the hypocrites 2 do in the synagogues and in the streets to win the praise of others. Amen, I say to you, they have received their reward. 3But when you give alms, do not let your left hand know what your right is doing" (Mt6, 2-3)

One aspect that Jesus shows us, and perhaps one of the most difficult to practice, is to forgive those who trespass against us, deceive, betray, or humiliate us.

He tells us that we not only ought to forgive them 70 times 7, that is, always; but that we must help them and love them. Yes, we must love even our enemies.

What merit do you have if you love only your friends who love you? That the publicans also do, who do not have faith. No, you must also love your enemies.

"44 But I tell you: Love your enemies and pray for your persecutors; 45 be sons of your Father in heaven, because he makes his sun rise on the evil and good and makes the rain fall on the just and unjust. 46 If you love those who love you, what recompense will you have? Do not the tax collectors do the same?"(Mt5, 44-46)

We can say, in general, that we are always consciously trying to be prepared for, when the Father calls us to the eternal abode.

We have preached to our children by words and personal example the way to practice and live our faith to the fullest.

Thus, we wanted them to learn that there should be consistency between what we say and what we do.

I wish to recommend you, very strongly, to dedicate your homes and families to the Two Hearts of Jesus and Mary.

We must remember the attacks on our Holy Mother Church and the decisions of leaders and politicians to ban religious practices; especially, in Christian schools and public places. These are very difficult times for Catholics.

Let us keep up steadfast in the practice of our faith!

We can be sure that the Lord Jesus Christ and the Blessed Mother will always protect us.

The now Blessed John Paul II, told us:

"It is fitting at this time, seek greater depth and awareness of the intimate relationship between the Two Hearts and the value to our day, a true devotion and consecration to the Hearts of Jesus and Mary" (Pope John Paul II, November 23, 1987)

The blessings on our home have been so many and so abundant that we can only say:

THANK YOU, BELOVED FATHER!

THANK YOU, JESUS, MY LORD AND SAVIOR!

THANK YOU HOLY SPIRIT OF GOD!

THANK YOU, HOLY MOTHER!

THANK YOU SO MUCH!

CONCLUSION

My hope in writing this book was, and is, to give you some ideas that can make your marriage, that commitment for life, an experience not only enjoyable, but also, joyful and happy.

To make this a reality, it is necessary that each of the members of that family: wife, husband, and children, contribute their best for the good and happiness of each of the other components of the family.

Such collaboration, for the good of others, we must do it with true love.

It is good to remember here what St. Paul tells us in his letter to the Corinthians:

I can make all the sacrifices, give everything I own, and even give my own body, if I do not do it for love, I gain nothing, and adds:

"4 Love is patient and kind, love does not envy, it does not boast, it is not proud, 5 did not proceed with meanness, not seek its own interests, is not provoked, does not take into account a wrong suffered, 6 does not rejoice at wrongdoing, but rejoices with the truth. 7 It bears all things, believes all things, hopes all things, endures all things."(1Cor13, 4-7)

A healthier, happy, accomplished, and successful family is only achieved when everyone asks itself: Are those who live with me really happy? What can I do or change to make that a reality in my home?

I want to emphasize the most the following comment:

Although we create the ideal environment in our home for each of the members comprising it, we should not feel it a disappointment or a failure if some of our children, after reaching adulthood, behave at odds with what was taught and lived for so many years within the family.

I also remind you of all the social, cultural, and intrinsic factors of the person which affects everyone throughout life.

Family prayer and the prayer of each individually on a regular and permanent basis is the only safe guarantee of achieving the ideal home: financially solidly, happy, and healthy.

A home that is capable of creating the environment that promotes balanced, happy people that will contribute positively to the society in which they live and the world at large.

I left the following thought for this part of the book because I want it to stay engraved within the depths of us; that shapes all our actions and inactions; that affects our thinking and our priorities.

That helps us to set the goal, the main and final objective: to attain the crown of Glory with which the Lord awaits us at the end of our earthly life.

The reflection is the following: "All household members must understand that although we must address the meeting of our temporary needs, that our efforts should be focused on ensuring that every member of our family has, as their primary objective: the attainment of eternal life."

Remember what the Apostle James tells us: (we saw it before, but it is worth repeating):

"17So also faith of itself, if it does not have works, is dead.18Indeed someone might say, "You have faith and I have works." Demonstrate your faith to me without works, and I will demonstrate my faith to you from my works". (James 2, 17-18)

I have come to the conclusion that we came to this world for one purpose: to learn to love unconditionally as God loves us.

Frequent participation of the Sacraments of Penance and Eucharist, adoration of the Blessed Sacrament, regular reading of the Word of God, the continuous practice of the Holy Rosary, etc., are the ways that Jesus left us to live our faith in all its fullness; to put our faith into action, to ensure consistency between what we say and do.

At the end of our earthly lives, we will be examined on one subject, love, and within this, on a single topic: charity.

The Lord tells us:

"31[14] "When the Son of Man comes in his glory, and all the angels with him, he will sit upon his glorious throne,32and all the nations [15] will be assembled before him. And he will separate them one from another, as a shepherd separates the sheep from the goats.33He will place the sheep on his right and the goats on his left.34Then the king will say to those on his right, 'Come, you who are blessed by my Father. Inherit the kingdom prepared for you from the foundation of the world.35For I was hungry and you gave me food, I was thirsty and you gave me drink, a stranger and you welcomed me,36naked and you clothed me, ill and you cared for me, in prison and you visited me.'37Then the righteous [16] will answer him and say, 'Lord, when did we see you hungry and feed you, or thirsty and give you drink?38When did we see you a stranger and welcome you, or naked and clothe you?39When did we see you ill or in prison, and visit you?'40And the king will say to them in reply, 'Amen, I say to you, whatever you did for one of these least brothers of mine, you did for me.'41[17] Then he will say to those on his left, 'Depart from me, you accursed, into the eternal fire prepared for the devil and his angels.42For I was hungry and you gave me no food, I was thirsty and you gave me no drink,43a stranger and you gave me no welcome, naked and you gave me no clothing, ill and in prison, and you did not care for me.'44[18] Then they will answer and say, 'Lord, when did we see you hungry or thirsty or a stranger or naked or ill or in prison, and not minister to your needs?'45He will answer them, 'Amen, I say to you, what you did not do for one of these least ones, you did not do for me.'46And these will go off to eternal punishment, but the righteous to eternal life."(Mt25, 31-46)

Remember, in everything you do, do it always as if it only depended on our capabilities and activities; but, do it with such a faith and confidence as if it only depended on God.

To do ourselves everything we can and trust fully in God should be our motto in life.

I conclude this book with the prayer for the family said by the Holy Father Pope Benedict XVI:

"Oh, God, who in the Holy Family left us a perfect model of family life, lived in faith and obedience to your will.

Help us be an example of faith and love for your commandments.

Help us in our mission of transmitting the faith to our children. Open their hearts to grow in them the seed of faith received in Baptism.

Strengthen the faith of our youth to grow in knowledge of Jesus. Increase love and faithfulness in all marriages, especially those going through times of suffering or difficulty.

United to Joseph and Mary, We ask this through Jesus Christ your Son, our Lord, Amen." (Prayer for the family prayed for His Holiness Benedict XVI at the V World Meeting of Families, City of Arts and Sciences, Valencia, Spain. Saturday July 8, 2006)

For my part I ask blessings: to our Lord Jesus Christ, God and Savior; to the Blessed Virgin Mary, our Mother in Heaven and our beloved Saint Joseph, for each of you and your families.

BIBLIOGRAPHY

1. THE BOOK OF THE PEOPLE OF GOD, THE BIBLE, ARGENTINA'S TRANSLATION, 1990.

2. CATECHISM OF THE CATHOLIC CHURCH.

3. THEOLOGY OF THE BODY: GENERAL AUDIENCES OF HIS HOLINESS, THE BLESSED JOHN PAUL II, FROM SEPTEMBER 5, 1979 TO NOVEMBER 8, 1984.

INDEX

MARRIAGE, A decision for life 3

ECCLESIASTIC LICENSE 5

DEDICATION 6

ACKNOWLEDGMENTS 7

FOREWORD.. 9

THE SACRAMENT OF MARRIAGE 14

INTRODUCTION.. 17

Chapter I. YOU, AS A HUMAN BEING 21

Chapter II: PREPARING FOR MARRIAGE 33

Chapter IIa: PREPARATION FOR PRODUCTIVE LIFE.................................... 40

Chapter IIb: SEARCH FOR THE SPOUSE. CONTINUATION OF THE PREPARATION 46

Chapter III. COURTSHIP, CONTINUATION OF THE PREPARATION 55

Chapter IV.THE MARRIAGE, A DECISION FOR LIFE 63

Chapter IVa. COMMUNICATION BETWEEN THE COUPLE AND AT HOME 68

Chapter IVb. THEKNOWLEDGE OF YOUR PARTNER AND THE TREATMENT
BETWEEN THE TWO 73

Chapter IVc. SEXUAL INTIMACY.. 82

Chapter IVd. THE TEMPTATIONS 100

Chapter IVe. THE HOME ENVIROMENT AND ITS INFLUENCE IN THE
DEVELOPMENT AND PERSONALITY OF CHILDREN...................................... 105

Chapter IVf. OPEN TO LIFE 134

Chapter IVg. THE BIG MISTAKE 140

Chapter IVh. MONEY AND THE FAMILY 145

Chapter IVi. FAMILY PRAYER.. 163

CONCLUSION 174

BIBLIOGRAFY 180

INDEX.. 181

www.ingramcontent.com/pod-product-compliance
Lightning Source LLC
Chambersburg PA
CBHW030005110426
42736CB00040BA/407